IMMIGRANT GIRL, RADICAL WOMAN

IMMIGRANT GIRL,

WITH COMMENTARY AND ORIGINAL DRAWINGS
BY **ROBBIN LÉGÈRE HENDERSON**

*

AFTERWORD BY **ILEEN A. DEVAULT**

RADICAL WOMAN

A MEMOIR FROM THE EARLY
TWENTIETH CENTURY

*

MATILDA RABINOWITZ

ILR PRESS • AN IMPRINT OF **CORNELL UNIVERSITY PRESS**

ITHACA AND LONDON

First published 2017 by Cornell University Press

Printed in the United States of America

Library of Congress Cataloging-in-Publication Data
Names: Rabinowitz, Matilda, 1887–1963, author.
| Henderson, Robbin, commentator, illustrator. |
DeVault, Ileen A., writer of afterword.
Title: Immigrant girl, radical woman : a memoir from
the early twentieth century / Matilda Rabinowitz ;
with commentary and original drawings by Robbin
Légère Henderson ; afterword by Ileen A. DeVault.
Description: Ithaca : ILR Press, an imprint of Cornell
University Press, 2017. | Includes bibliographical
references and index.
Identifiers: LCCN 2017006130| ISBN 9781501709845
(pbk. : alk. paper) | ISBN 9781501709487 (pdf)
Subjects: LCSH: Rabinowitz, Matilda, 1887–1963. |
Women in the labor movement—United States—
Biography. | Women immigrants—United States—
Biography. | Jewish women—United States-—
Biography. | Labor unions—Organizing—United
States—History—20th century. | Industrial Workers
of the World—Biography. | Socialist Party (U.S.)—
Biography.
Classification: LCC HD8073.R33 R33 2017 | DDC
331.88/6092 [B] —dc23
LC record available at https://lccn.loc.gov/2017006130

Cornell University Press strives to use environmentally responsible suppliers and materials to the fullest extent possible in the publishing of its books. Such materials include vegetable-based, low-VOC inks and acid-free papers that are recycled, totally chlorine-free, or partly composed of nonwood fibers. For further information, visit our website at cornellpress.cornell.edu.

CONTENTS

PREFACE

Matilda called it simply "My Story," but at the beginning it could have been the story of hundreds of thousands of immigrant girls who arrived in America around the turn of the twentieth century. She says she wrote this story for my brothers and me, her grandchildren, but I have felt for years that it should be more widely known, because her life represents the lives of many immigrant girls who dreamed that America would provide a better life than the one they had escaped—those who found toil, exploitation, and disappointment, yet struggled to realize the ideals of democracy, freedom, and equality that drew them here.

How much more danger she faced than I have ever known—and confusion. How hard was her daily toil, how great her fear, and how brave her choices. As I read the manuscript over and over, I continue to marvel at Matilda's courage and the strength of her gifts. But, as with all memoir, lacunae occur and questions arise. I am grateful for what she tells us but curious about what is omitted. I wonder about the distortions, the misremembrances, the hidden truths, the missing chapters in her story. I want to present this emblematic story as it was written. But I also want to contribute my feelings, insights, and discoveries. Over the years, I have done extensive research and visited almost all the places she mentions. In searching for her, I look for my roots—our roots—as women, activists, mothers, and lovers. Her thirst for beauty, her demand for justice, her need for connection and

meaning through comrades, friends, and the family she founded mirrors the dreams and desires of generations of her sisters—and mine.

I adored my "Nana." She was an attentive grandma, smart, engaged, and creative. She played games with us and made up bedtime stories when we were little, and as we grew, she energetically engaged our varied views on current events, history, and politics. As I have learned more about her life through her words and the work of those who shared those times with her—from scholars of labor history, women's history, and the politics of the twentieth century—I come to see her, not only as my "Nana," but as "Matilda," one who belongs to all of us. I begin to know her as a figure of history who participated in shaping the social and political forces in America, changes that have benefited me and the generations to come—worker's rights, women's emancipation, economic and racial equity.

I remember my grandmother sitting at her little desk in front of the big Corona typewriter, rapidly tapping the keys and shifting the carriage with a ping. But I knew little of her early life in Russia, her journey to America, or her contribution to the history of labor. Only on reading her memoir did I learn that she crossed the Atlantic in a ship so unseaworthy that it was decommissioned in the year following the voyage. Although my brothers and I knew about our mother's unusual upbringing, I had not understood the courage it took to decide deliberately to bring a child into the world in the early twentieth century without a husband or family support. As I discovered my grandmother through the pages of her memoir, others were finding her, too.

Philip S. Foner, in his *Women and the American Labor Movement*,* describes Matilda as "middle class." She would have rejected this representation. Her narrative of the precarious livelihood in the Pale, the family traveling steerage to America, the fourth-class trains and

*New York: Free Press, 1979-80.

surreptitious border crossings, and the time it took her father to accumulate half the funds to bring the family across the Atlantic are not the memories of a middle-class girl. Although she loved language and literature, she had only an eighth-grade education. Instead of attending school, she lived in tenements and worked in sweatshops and factories from the age of thirteen.

To be sure, her mother's family, innkeepers in the Russian Ukraine, may have been petit bourgeois at one time, but she describes their struggle to provide a living for an extended family. It was not dire poverty, but it was hardly middle class. And they were Jews in the Pale where there were few employment options—artisans, craftsmen, peddlers, or small businesspeople were their lot. Many of the men were unemployed or underemployed. Her father, a rabbinical scholar, was an artisan from a family of craftspeople—a machinist in America.

It is often assumed that the IWW was an anarchist organization, often called "anarcho-syndicalist." Matilda would reject this description of her views. Although a syndicalist, she was a Socialist always (even when she left the party), and she found anarchism "romantic." She dismissed Filippo Bocchini, our grandfather's codefendant in Little Falls, as just such a romantic anarchist.

More recently she has begun to be "rediscovered" by scholars and writers interested in the labor movement and women's history. The labor historian and feminist scholar Joyce Shaw Peterson's sensitive discussion of Matilda's decision to have a child on her own* reminded me of a story my grandmother told me when I was probably nineteen or twenty. Sometime in the early 1920s, in the first year of my mother's life, Matilda bobbed her hair and took her baby to visit a cousin. Opening the door to them, the relative shrank back hissing, "I don't like Bolshevik haircuts, and I don't like Bolshevik babies!" and slammed the door. We laughed and

*Joyce Shaw Peterson, "Matilda Robbins: A Woman's Life in the Labor Movement, 1900–1920," *Labor History* 34:1 (1993), 33–56.

laughed that day nearly fifty years later, but at the time the rejection would have been deeply felt.

Terry Judd, a Detroit-area journalist, generously shared his research on the auto industry, sending articles about Matilda he found in the Detroit Library archives. There were news photos of her speaking—tiny Matilda standing on a crate, barely as tall as the men listening—then of her subsequent arrest. On a visit to Detroit, I spent days sifting through Ben's and Matilda's papers in the Walter Reuther Library at Wayne State University. Terry offered to show me "Matilda's Detroit," one hundred years after she led the first auto industry strike. One of our stops was the Model T Museum.

Sometimes my search for Matilda yielded interactions with people that were uncomfortable, if not hostile. That notorious anti-Semite Henry Ford detested unions. In fact, some historians credit Matilda's efforts at Studebaker with forcing Ford, fearing unionization, to increase his workers' salaries to five dollars a day. My friend Terry answered the query about what brought us to the Model T Museum to a seemingly friendly docent; the museum is still located next to the site where the Studebaker factory stood one hundred years ago. Terry introduced me as the granddaughter of the leader of the first auto industry strike. The now unkindly docent sneered, "And you're PROUD of that?" Unions are as unpopular today among most workers as they were among the captains of industry in her day. Now vast numbers of poorly paid workers who consider themselves "middle class" have been persuaded that unions are useless and corrupt, not recognizing that organized labor created our country's middle class.

Encounters with writers and historians and my travels to many of the places mentioned in Matilda's memoir, especially those places where Matilda struggled to improve labor conditions, help me imagine her. She was a young woman, under five feet tall, a bold speaker and passionate fighter for working people's rights. They help me see some of the landscape that was the background to her life, and I feel her presence.

Matilda's account mixes reticence and candor. Her mind brimming with political ardor and romantic passion, she was a Victorian-era woman and a twentieth-century rebel in a small body. She was modest, but she could be fierce in an argument. Whether poetry, expository essays, or fiction, her art, based in experience, was literary. We are the beneficiaries of what she observed and participated in and what she wrote. We see in her struggle the struggles of all the others whose voices are lost to us. Reading her writing, recalling her as she was, and discovering the records others have kept and compiled has given me a critical opportunity as a woman, granddaughter, and artist to bring her to life for a new audience.

Matilda's unique contribution is the written testimony. With all its omissions and opacity, I am grateful for her story. May it inform and inspire others, as it has me.

ACKNOWLEDGMENTS

Thanks to my guide, Louis Baum, and my host, Jayne Ritz, both of Little Falls, New York, and to members of the Little Falls Historical Society, whose beautiful, historically rigorous centennial commemoration of the strike of 1912–13 inspired in me a serious effort to bring Matilda's manuscript to a wider audience.

I am grateful to the historian Joyce Shaw Peterson, whose research on Matilda showed me the importance of this story and impelled my work. Thanks also to William LeFevre, senior archivist, and Mary Wallace, audiovisual archivist, at the Walter P. Reuther Library, Wayne State University, for their careful attention during my hours at the archives. Special thanks to Terry Judd, the Detroit-area journalist, who sent me newspaper images he found, along with text featuring Matilda during the Studebaker strike of 1913, and for his generosity in devoting a day to show me a thoroughly researched tour of "Matilda's Detroit."

To my dear friend Mary Thomas Apodaca, guide to the "gallant south," companion and driver in my quest to find what is left of Matilda's Greenville, South Carolina: the old mills and mill villages where Matilda faced her "toughest job."

Stephen R. Thornton, of the Shoeleather History Project, and Andy Piascik, author, introduced me to Matilda's Bridgeport and helped me gain access to archives where we found the locations of her family's home and the corset factories where she sweated so I could visit them.

The staff of the Nantucket Historical Association Research Library helped me find an early location of the Cottage Hospital where Matilda gave birth to my mother in 1919; they also pointed the way to the presumed location of the cabin and the nearby home of her friends, Phyllis and Jay Cisco, where Matilda and her baby spent that summer.

Thanks also to my New Hampshire friends Mark and Tina Leary, who provided shelter on my way to the Brick House in Mill Hollow, East Alstead.

Thanks to the Puffin Foundation, which supported an exhibition of these drawings, and to the Blue Mountain Center, a perfect environment for work and stimulating conversation, where I finished drawings and text. I am grateful also to Renny Pritikin, chief curator at the Contemporary Jewish Museum in San Francisco, and Nancy Mizuno Elliott, gallery director and professor at City College of San Francisco, who brought the drawings to public attention in two separate exhibitions.

Harry Siitonen, the last of Matilda's Wobbly comrades, collected and offered his copies of the *Socialist Newsletter* (Los Angeles), where my grandmother contributed a regular column, as well as shared with me his memories of Matilda. For his attentiveness to her when she lived, and for maintaining contact with her family since her death, *kiitos.*

To Bob Schildgen, friend and excellent editor, thanks for numerous readings of various parts and versions of this manuscript, embarrassment-saving suggestions, and sage counsel. Thanks also to Frances Benson, acquisitions editor, and to all the editors and designers at ILR Press and Cornell University Press. I'm grateful for your support, guidance, and care in producing this book.

To Michael Schwartz, the instigator of this book, thanks for getting the ball rolling. It is great to have influential friends. My gratitude also to Cecilia Brunazzi and the Nancys, Buchanan and Ippolito, dear friends, sensitive and critical readers, providers of suggestions and encouragement.

To my brother Mark Scott Henderson and his wife, Yolanda

Vigil-Henderson, engaged supporters; my brother Dal, fellow artist and generous critic of my drawings; and my middle brother, Eric, our academic one; and sisters-in-law Suzanne and Amy—for your love and encouragement, thank you. To them and the rest of our family—my children, Daromir Rudnyckyj and Xenia Rudnycka, eight nieces and nephews, and the next generation: my three grandchildren and four greatnieces and -nephews (Matilda's great-great-grandchildren)—love and solidarity forever.

My love and gratitude to Jos Sances, boon companion, bold artist, master printer, loving critic, and ever-supportive helpmeet. Thanks for sharing the journey.

IMMIGRANT GIRL, RADICAL WOMAN

1   THESE WERE PIONEERS, TOO

When my mother left the Ukraine with her five children to join my father in New York it was her third trip away from the small town of Litin where she and many generations of her forebears were born. Her first trip was to her husband's town, Shargorod, about 20 miles away, when she was a young bride. Her second trip was to a nearby town to which the family thought of moving, but didn't. And now to America.

The year was 1900. My father had been gone five years. He had spent a year in London. Then he moved on to New York and what he hoped was more opportunity to earn money and bring his family over. It took four years to scrape together enough to pay down one-half of the fare for one full and four half tickets (the youngest child being only five went free) from Russia to New York by fourth-class railroad and ship steerage. The other half, guaranteed by his lodge members, was to be met in weekly installments out of his future wages.

Naturally my mother was terrified at the prospect of traveling. The whole world was alien, and she was going to an alien land. But go she must. And so the day of departure arrived, a day of mourning. The family, the little town, the associations, for all the poverty and the cruelty of the Pale, had been all she had in life. Here she had been a young bride in a yellow silk dress, standing under the marriage canopy with her handsome groom. Here her children had been born.

Many were the lean years. Great had often been her terror of persecution and pogrom, but it was the only home she knew. The only home we knew.

I was 12, the eldest. And once I, too, had made the journey to Shargorod to see for the first time my paternal grandfather and my step-grandmother. My father's mother died when he was born.

I remember the springless wagon and the clumsy lean horses. Three boards, slightly above the floor of the wagon, were fitted to its sides for seats. There was straw on the floor, and on the seats strips of old gray felt. I was the smallest passenger and in the charge of an adult acquaintance who was traveling somewhere beyond Shargorod. The wagon bumped over the rutty roads at about two miles an hour, and it took almost a day to make the journey.

It was just such a wagon that gathered us up to start the journey to America. There were six of us and two young men who were going the 30 odd miles with us to the nearest railroad at the town of Vinnitsa. Our baggage, packed in sacking, was squeezed into the rear of the wagon and tied with ropes. My mother carried a basket of food, and there was also an especially heavy linen sack with slices of rye bread, soaked in beer and dried. Eaten with tea this would often make a meal on our long journey. There were also goose cracklings, very dry, in an earthen crock wrapped securely in sacking and packed in a basket. How we later appreciated this delicacy when food was scarce on board ship! Lemons were each carefully wrapped in sacking and put in with apples in a coarse linen bag. This was all the food we took; it was only intended to supplement the other food we would get on the way. Little did my mother dream how basic and precious it all would turn out to be, as our journey stretched into many weeks.

The wagon stood in front of my grandfather's house on what was the main street of the town. The street was wide, unpaved, rutty. In the spring it was a stream of mud, in the summer inches of dust, in the fall mud again, and in the winter covered by snow and sleet. It was lined with ugly one-story wooden houses, set close to each other, without gardens or shade trees. There was a kind of a boardwalk that ran along the front of the houses the length of the street for about 300 yards and then ended abruptly in ragged bushes and weeds. And beyond was the river, a small, sluggish, but rather clear, stream.

The opposite side of the street had fewer houses, unpainted, rickety. The spaces between were wider, and in them were set up crude stalls where women sold flour, herring, dried fish, apples, and other fruit in season. Some of the houses had cellars that were occupied by shoemakers, tinsmiths, coopers, carpenters, and other craftsmen. There was always activity on that side: the tap-tap of the shoemakers; the distinct hammer of the carpenter; the clang of copper and tin.

On warm days the women dozed at their wares. Sometimes there was a sad awakening as a dog snatched a fish, or a pig on the loose would upset a trough. Then several women would jump up and take after the animal. The craftsmen would pop out of their doors in commiseration and sympathy, and I would hear imprecations and doleful comments. "Sad, how sad life is! How hard it is to make a living! So much struggle for a piece of bread!"

My maternal grandparents ran a kind of combination liquor store and tearoom. The large front room of their house contained shelves where the bottled vodka with its government seal was displayed. The stock was meager, and my uncles, young men in their twenties, were always running out for more stock. The tearoom part was in the hands of my grandmother and my two aunts, both younger than their

brothers. They served mostly fish, both hot and cold, and tea. Ordinarily there were rarely more than four people, usually peasants in from the country, eating at the long pine table. But on days when a company of soldiers was going through the town, or when recruiting was going on, the place was full. The liquor could be opened and drunk outside only. But there was quite a bit of swigging going on at the table from a small bottle.

How could that family of seven, all adults except the youngest, live on the small proceeds of the business? There was no other income. My uncles were fairly well educated, but trained for nothing useful. They gave lessons in reading and writing, one in Yiddish, the other in Russian, at 50 kopeks a lesson. There were, however, few lessons. Most educated Jewish young men and women tried to give lessons,

and too few could afford them. One of my aunts, the younger one, not quite twenty, was well versed in Hebrew. Whatever her aspirations were, teaching could not have been one of them. For women did not teach Hebrew in that little town—Russian, yes, but not Hebrew. That was restricted to men, regardless of how ill equipped they may have been for it. There was nothing for women to do outside the home; the scant business of the tearoom was the only work there was. The girls just waited to be married.

My grandfather was short, but well formed, with rather handsome features, prematurely gray, and an almost white beard. Years later when he came to the United States and I was grown, I remember thinking how much like a Goya portrait he looked. The family name was Schpanier (Spaniards). He seemed to do the least in the way of making a living. He attended to his prayers morning and evening. He slept a lot after the midday dinner and went to bed early after the evening meal. The hours between he just sat—outside in fine weather, inside near the clay stove when it was cold. There were long hours in the synagogue on the Sabbath, which started with sundown Friday and ended with sundown Saturday, and longer hours of sleep. He lived to be 90.

My grandmother was somewhat taller than my grandfather, also rather good-looking, but with a Slavic cast of feature. She was more energetic than my grandfather. With the two girls she did all the managing of the food business: baking all the bread and cooking and salting and freezing of fish. They also made their own clothes, except those for important occasions such as weddings, when more professional service was called for. The girls and my grandmother, too, indeed the whole family was always decently dressed. And for holidays there were usually new outfits for all. And again I wondered in later years how they managed on such pittance of an income.

The Russian Orthodox Church stood opposite my grandfather's house. It was surrounded by a high fence made of birch logs, the bark left natural. It all but hid the structure below the dome, which was painted blue and gold and was topped by three gilded crosses. The yard had trees in it, birch and aspen, and lilac bushes that were lovely in the spring. From the roof of my grandfather's house I could look right into the churchyard and watch the religious processions with the ikons and banners and censors as they went round and round, the priest and acolytes chanting. On the awesome Friday I could see the whole ritual of burying the crucified figure, and I continued to watch in fascination the whole three-day vigil with the chanting and praying. Then early Easter Sunday I could hear the paean and singing of Christ has Risen! Christ has Risen! The peasants would pour in

from the country for the day-long services. There would be no stalls on that day on the street, but the next day would be a busy one of trade, barter, and drinking. Trade for the artisans was brisk as the peasants brought their boots to be mended, their tin samovars to be soldered, their saws and other tools to be sharpened. Easter week was a great trading week in the town. The peasants brought their winter produce to town: homespun, sheepskins, flax, woodenware to exchange for tea, sugar, hardware, calico, crude oil, whatever they could afford for their primitive household and farm needs. They slept wrapped in their sheepskins in their wagons on the outskirts of the town, and sometimes during the night I could hear their singing. My grandparents' business was more brisk during these days, and my grandmother would be more short-tempered from overwork.

When my father left Russia in search of a living in foreign lands, I was about eight. He slipped out without a passport and made his way to London. There he worked for over a year in a candy factory at a weekly wage of a pound. Out of this he sent something home. How little it must have been! In the United States he worked at various semiskilled jobs in the metal trade in New York. His earnings were still low and the contribution to the family no greater, as he was saving toward the expenses of bringing us over.

We lived on the edge of poverty. Bread, potatoes, cabbage, and beet soup were our staple diet all winter. There was little meat. In the summer there was the variety of fresh vegetables, cucumbers, peas, corn, squash. Cherries and plums were in abundance. Jam was made and plum butter for the winter. Apples and pears came in the fall, and apples lasted all winter; we ate them frozen, as well. It was a meager living.

Our housing as far back as I could remember was poor. My earliest recollection is of a basement apartment, adjacent to an inn. I was probably five then. My father had been an agent for some years for liquor dealers who provisioned the military, but was squeezed out by another. He then engaged in retail beer selling, and the front room of our home was the salesroom. My mother tried to run the business after my father left Russia but found it too strenuous and unsafe for a woman. During the early years of their marriage, however, my parents must have been in better circumstances. For they were able to employ a nurse for the three of us older children. Of course, a peasant nurse in those days in Russia probably received a meager sum—three rubles a month, or something like that, and her room and board. But

even so, it meant that they had been better off at one time. I remember our nurse as a gentle little body who was devoted to us. I still remember some of the songs she sang to us.

Although the family lived in the rear of the salesroom, I do not remember crowding or discomfort. It was after my father left that I was aware of the smallness of our quarters. My mother and the children, now five of us, usually occupied two rented rooms, one larger that was both a living and a sleeping room and a kitchen where cooking and eating and washing would go on during the day and where one of the three boys slept. The two younger boys had a bed in the living room. My mother, my little sister, and I occupied the other bed. It was crowded living, and I resented the lack of privacy as a child and always. It was from this dwelling that we set out for America.

I was sent to school at an early age, officially at seven, as one could not enter before. But from remarks that I recall here and there by members of the family it would seem that I had gone earlier. At any rate, I graduated from what would be the equivalent of an American grade school at 12.

The schools in Russia were government subsidized and controlled,

under the strict supervision of local authorities. There was a small
yearly fee, as near as I can remember around six rubles a year. I had
the same teacher in the Russian and ancient Slavonic language for the
five years that I was at the school. The Slavonic, the language of the
Russian Orthodox Church as Latin is of the Catholic Church, was a
great bore. It was apparently taught us only for the purpose of reading
religious texts. At any rate, I don't remember reading anything else
in it. But we had to make a passing grade in it along with the other
subjects: history, geography, arithmetic, and penmanship.

The sexes were segregated with a tall board fence between the play
yards. The language teacher was also the girls' supervisor. She was a
harsh old maid and a bitter anti-Semite. To the usual punishments
for infractions imposed on all the Jewish children she added slurs
and insults. There was no redress and no alternative to this school. It
was only recently that girls were even considered fit to be educated by
their families. Traditionally they were maintained in ignorance, since
the duties of a wife did not include any necessity for education. It was
the only public school, and private tutors were not for people in our
economic condition.

There was no high school in Litin, although it was a town of around 10,000 and the county seat. So after graduation there was nothing for me to do but wait until we were ready to leave for America, which was not to be for almost a year. So I read, and I read, and I tried to learn German in a desultory way. I spent much time with a chum, who graduated with me although she was two years older. She was preparing herself to go to the gymnasium in a larger town. We read a lot of poetry together and walked and yearned, as adolescents will. Her father and mother were both hatters who turned out modes for the gentry in their shop at home. I admired their beautiful craft, but my friend and her older sister were bent on intellectual pursuits. The education Jewish children were able to obtain under the restrictions imposed on them—only a small number could enter the gymnasia and fewer still the universities—brought little social or financial gain. They were excluded from civil service, restricted in the professions, and there was too little industry to offer any appreciable opportunities to the six million Jewish subjects of the czar. Petty business and general huckstering was the lot of most. The artisans, even the best, were considered low caste by their brethren, those who tormented their brains in an effort to eke out a living.

There was absolutely nothing in which the children of the petty tradesmen or artisans who had gotten any sort of education could engage in my town. Some few went on to larger places to struggle for more education; a few, not many, learned the trades of their fathers. But most just lived on the parents, as my uncles did, growing into manhood and deteriorating, feeling superior to the tailors and shoemakers and tinsmiths.

The more adventurous emigrated, some to Germany or to England, but mostly to the United States. In the 1880s began that trek of the Russian, Polish, Romanian, and Galician Jews that brought millions out of these benighted lands, that created new ghettoes in the large American cities, that enslaved tens of thousands in sweatshops, and that led, three or four decades later, to the unionization of the needle trades and clothing industry.

My father came from a family of artisans. His father had been a harness maker, and the uncle in whose home he grew up was a famed coppersmith in his province. As a boy my father wanted to follow the trade of his uncle, but his aunt, who adored him, wanted him to be a Hebrew scholar. The son of her only sister, who had died in childbirth, was just too good to be a craftsman. But for all the interference, my father did gain considerable skill in metalwork, and he had a real appreciation of fine handicraft. The dowry that my mother brought him was in recognition of his Hebrew scholarship, not of his potential as a craftsman. Since he married into a family with a petty liquor business though, my father perforce participated in the business. He never had ambition for it, however, and my mother resented his ineptitude. To the end of his life he remained inept as a businessman.

The government's increasing control of the liquor trade, which had been largely in the hands of Jews living in the Pale, further curtailed my family's means of livelihood. The government required that all liquor must be bottled, and a heavier tax was now imposed on its sale. Naturally sales fell. Little hostelries, like those of my grandparents, that sold food along with vodka were hard pressed. The struggle to eke out a living became ever more intense. There were two grown sons and two marriageable daughters. The sons looked for wives, hoping to marry into families that would set them up at some means of making a living. The two girls, both very good-looking, and one of them very bright, saw little future for themselves without dowries. My third uncle, only two years older than I, was still in school. Yet the family was decently clad, there was white bread for the Sabbath and special

food and sweetmeats and raisin wine. How was it done from the little profit on the bottled vodka, the jellied fish, which my grandmother prepared and sold, the cheese and chopped liver turnovers that the peasants bought on weekly market days? Millions of Jews lived thus, and even more poorly, under the czars.

My father, with the advent of the liquor monopoly, lost his commission to supply liquor to the military club and left for America sometime in 1895. He had a distant relative in London, and he had no money to go on. So there he remained for a year, cutting candy at a pound a week.

MATILDA LOVED TO TELL HER GRANDCHILDREN BED-time stories; a favorite was about two children, Hannah and Dan, just the ages of my brother Dal and me. The fictional children lived in New Hampshire on a farm—exotic tales for children who were reared in urban Los Angeles. My brother and I liked the stories, especially the winter tales of tapping maple trees for the sweet sap and eating snowballs dredged in their syrup. "Now tell us about when you were a little girl in Russia, Nana," we begged, but she deflected our curiosity, preferring to tell us about these happy American children living a healthy, rural life. These stories were based on her memory of the scant year she spent in East Alstead, New Hampshire, following the birth of our mother.

Over the years, I have come to realize that in spite of her child-hood curiosity, love of language, and deep affection for the natural world, most of Matilda's memories of her early years involved feelings of anxiety, loss, privation, and alienation. She wanted to spare us sad stories deemed unsuitable bedtime stories for young children. Ever careful to protect our sensitivities, she even changed the lyrics of "Three Blind Mice." The farmer's wife didn't "cut off their tails with a carving knife"; she "cut them some cheese."

When I learned about the May Laws, I began to understand the reasons for the family's increasingly difficult livelihood. Enacted by Czar Alexander III, five years before Matilda was born, these laws designed to regulate the lives of Jews were said to be temporary measures, but they remained in effect for more than thirty years. These provisions affected the family's ability to thrive and gravely restricted their freedom.

The May Laws read as follows:

(1) As a temporary measure, and until a general revision is made of their legal status, it is decreed that the Jews be forbidden to settle anew outside of towns and boroughs, exceptions being admitted only in the case of existing Jewish agricultural colonies.

(2) Temporarily forbidden are the issuing of mortgages and other deeds to Jews, as well as the registration of Jews as lessees of real property situated outside of towns and boroughs; and also the issuing to Jews of powers of attorney to manage and dispose of such real property.

(3) Jews are forbidden to transact business on Sundays and on the principal Christian holy days; the existing regulations concerning the closing of places of business belonging to Christians on such days to apply to Jews also.

(4) The measures laid down in paragraphs 1, 2, and 3 shall apply only to the governments within the Pale of Jewish Settlement.*

Further laws were enacted the year Matilda was born, restricting education, imposing quotas on Jewish students within the Pale to 10 percent and then to 5 percent outside the Pale. In Moscow and Kiev, the quota was 3 percent. Doctors in the military were restricted to 5 percent, and lawyers needed consent from the minister of justice to practice at the bar. Nevertheless, Jewish men and boys were conscripted into the czar's armies, often by force.

These laws simply codified the Jewish second-class status that had been informally in place since the reign of Catherine the Great. Jews were not allowed into civil service, and their educational opportunities were always limited.

Matilda vividly describes the "Pale [of Settlement]," that area to which Jews were confined under the May Laws; the next generation would have called the area the "shtetl," a word I never heard her use.

The Pale comprised about 20 percent of Imperial Russia. The restrictions on movement and professions open to Jews, on owning land, and on doing business on Christian holy days diminished the ability to survive for a family dependent on serving snacks, tea, and especially liquor to peasants, the military, and townsfolk. Then, in 1891, the Jews' right to sell liquor was completely revoked. Four years after this, his ability to provide for his family further restricted, her father was gone, off to England, then to America where—with his lodge** lending him half the money—he eventually saved enough to send for his family.

*Herman Rosenthal, "May Laws," *Jewish Encyclopedia* online, http://www.jewish encyclopedia.com/articles/10508-may-laws.

**Almost all Jewish men who immigrated in those years joined lodges, or clubs comprised of "landsmen," men from their region. These brotherhoods were informal lending institutions as well as social clubs where politics, religion, and news of the day would be exchanged.

She loved learning—reading, reciting, knowing—but it was difficult for a serious, diligent student in Matilda's situation. Being Jewish and a girl, no matter how hard she strove, the rewards of a good education would no doubt have been out of reach. It would have been exceptional, unimaginable even, that she would be one of the 3 percent allowed to study in Kiev or Moscow, even had she been a boy. Still she expected to matriculate to the gymnasium, had she stayed in Russia. For a Jewish girl born in a European backwater in the nineteenth century, the May Laws severely limited educational opportunities.

Matilda complained of her mother's harshness, but the family's increase nearly every two years, intensifying the crowding and toil of caring for them while also helping with the family's declining business, undoubtedly was stressful and frightening for Bertha with her husband an unfathomable distance away. Matilda's beloved father, gentle and tender, was in America saving enough money to bring the family over. Bertha, caring for five young children, and helping in the family business, did not read or write, since girls of her generation and class were not expected to be educated. She was trained to cook, clean, sew, and piously observe Jewish custom and law. She wore the sheitel,* kept a kosher home, observed the dietary restrictions, and took the mikva, the monthly ritual bath required of all Jewish women. Her only expectation for her daughter was that she marry well and become a good housekeeper and a mother to as many children as God bestowed on her. Training Matilda in the domestic arts was meant to help achieve that pinnacle of female aspiration. In spite of her training, Matilda never enjoyed cooking, regarding it as a task to be borne and, if possible, shared with others. Affected by literature and history, yearning for beauty and meaning in her life, even though a good housekeeper and an expert needlewoman, Matilda cast her own hopes and dreams outside the sphere of domesticity.

My mother, Vita, told the story of staying alone in a New York

---

*A *sheitel* is a wig worn by Orthodox Jewish women who cut or shaved their hair upon marriage.

apartment one cold Friday evening as dusk was drawing near with Matilda's mother, a grandmother she rarely saw. Matilda may have been at work, or out and delayed for some reason. Vita was about five years old. Bertha spoke only Yiddish, which her grandchild didn't understand, but it was getting cold, the sun had set, and she made Vita understand that she wanted her to strike a match for the gas-fired heater. The little girl was shocked and frightened. She had been taught not to play with matches, and she had never lit a fire before. The only thing Bertha really understood about her daughter was that she had turned her back on the faith and traditions of her parents. Since the old woman was prohibited from lighting fires or even turning on a light once the sun set on Sabbath eve, her granddaughter, though a very young child, was designated the "Shabbos goy."*

Matilda's earliest memories speak of genteel poverty and the alienation suffered by members of a despised minority, but she also took pride in her intellectual accomplishments and felt connection to the sights and sounds of home. She was fascinated with the Easter rituals she watched from the roof of her grandparents' house in the same way her anthropologist grandsons and great-grandson became students of the rites and rituals of the people in the societies they observe. Despite the structural discrimination and the anti-Semitism the family experienced, Matilda showed little judgment of, only interest in, the Christian rituals.

When we children were growing up in Los Angeles, we had a neighbor, Daria Ivanovna, who spoke only Russian. My brother Dal and I were amazed one day to hear Matilda conversing with Daria Ivanovna in a language we had never heard our grandmother use before. What was she saying? "I was speaking to her in Russian," Matilda told us. When our grandmother sang a Russian lullaby to us and later to our younger brothers, the lyrics were always in English.

---

*A Shabbos goy was a gentile, usually a boy, hired by Orthodox Jews, to perform tasks forbidden on the Sabbath, like lighting fires or candles (later, turning on electric lights, driving a car, etc.).

"Sleep my Baby, sleep my darling
Lullaby-bye-loo
Silently the moon comes creeping
And looks down on you."

Years later, when I studied Russian and found the original in a book of poems by Mikhail Lermontov, Matilda taught me to pronounce the Russian to the tune I had learned as a child:

Spimla dienits moy prekrasni
Bayooshki Bayoo
Teho smotret mysats yasni
Vkolibel tvoyou.

I imagine the nanny who Matilda warmly remembers singing this song, but probably a peasant girl was more familiar with Ukrainian folk songs than songs of the poet. Matilda must have sung the Lermontov lullaby to Vita when she was a child. For, when my mother was dying, I sang the Russian version to her, and spontaneously at the end of the song she whispered, "Ya liubliu tebya" (I love you). It was the only time, the day before she died, I ever heard my mother speak Russian. No doubt as she lay dying she recalled what Matilda whispered before she kissed her goodnight.

I never heard Matilda speak her first language, Yiddish. Was this because she rejected Bertha's domesticity, or was she ashamed of her mother's illiteracy? Or did she simply oppose the acceptance of traditional roles? Perhaps, to her, Yiddish symbolized acquiescence to those roles and ignorance of the written word. I remember her describing Yiddish to me as "a bastard language." Yiddish has been described as bastardized German, but many revel in the richness and subtlety of this dying language.

Matilda was more sympathetic and sensitive to her father. She described him as tender and gentle. He worked as a machinist in Bridgeport from 1906 until he died there in the 1930s. She was proud of his abilities as a craftsman and seemed almost to admire his poor head for business. She described her mother as interested in business and fearful of debt. Those are qualities I remember in my grandmother that must have been inherited. Matilda managed her modest income well and bought and sold small properties later in life, providing a moderate rental income to supplement social security.

Though she didn't dwell on it, Matilda remarked on more than one occasion that her parents' marriage was unhappy. They were quite different in temperament and aspirations—her father intellectual, hardworking, but not ambitious; her mother practical, religiously observant, illiterate, and anxious about money. How much did her observations and evaluation of her parents influence her decisions and choices regarding love and marriage?

2 THE JOURNEY TO AMERICA

At Vinnitsa we boarded a train on the southeastern division of the Ukraine, which was to take us to the border. What border? We had no idea. My mother knew nothing of borders and cared less. All she hoped for was that we could get safely out of Russia without being caught without passports and returned—perhaps even imprisoned. As for me, although I knew enough geography to tell one border from another, and our railroad tickets indicated a town near Romania, it seemed a long way from the border. Doubtless, it was a cover-up. My mother told the conductor that we were going to visit relatives. He didn't seem concerned that our baggage suggested a long stay. Perhaps the bribing, so common in Russia, had already started?

Late that night we were put off at a small town. A peasant was waiting for us with a wagon loaded partly with straw. Our smaller belongings were unloaded, and we crowded in with them. Apparently the rest of the baggage, bedding, the samovar, and other utensils were elsewhere. We were taken to an inn, a small ramshackle house. At the door we were met by a small, harried-looking man, who spoke to us in Yiddish and to the peasant in Ukrainian, telling him to return later. In a low, whitewashed room, dimly lit by a kerosene lamp, we were served tea. We ate our own dried bread and used our own sugar.

My mother and our host spoke in whispers, but I could hear that we were to be smuggled across the stream some yards beyond the house. My three brothers and little sister were asleep on benches along the wall, while my mother and I kept vigil and listened for the approach of the peasant's wagon.

It was pitch dark outside when he arrived at the door. There was no wagon. We were to walk the distance to the stream. The children were awakened. The peasant put most of our belongings into a gunny sack; my mother carried the food basket, and each of the older children carried something. We stumbled along in silence over rutted earth, a distance of probably no more than 50 yards. My mother carried my little sister part of the way. It was the end of October, and the night was chilly. Because we wore as much of our clothing as possible, to save carrying or losing it, we were sweating when we reached the bank of the stream.

In the black night the stream rippled a grayish light. It was probably no more than 20 yards across, and I could, or thought I could, see the opposite bank. We huddled together, hardly breathing. My little sister whimpered a little, but my mother drew her shawl closer around her head, and the sound was muffled. I do not remember how long we sat on the bank. It seemed a long time. Suddenly in the deep dark there was a white spot and the gentle sound of an oar. Soon a figure could be made out rowing toward us. The rowboat was brought against the bank with hardly a sound. And at the same time our

peasant emerged from nowhere. He motioned us to get into the boat, which was held steady by a young peasant who stood in it like a statue, clad in his white homespun. Quickly our luggage was slipped in, and the boat pushed off as soundlessly as it put in. In a few minutes we were on the other side and in Romania.

Since we left Litin sometime in October and did not arrive in New York until December 25, 1900, it must have taken more than two months for the journey. How did we travel from Romania? How and why did we get to Rotterdam, then by slow boat to Glasgow to make the longest route possible to New York? It is difficult for me after these many years (and indeed it has always been difficult) to find an answer. In crossing countries, plains, rivers, and mountains we were shifted and shunted from one wretched train to another, from one miserable station to another. We spent days waiting for connections, huddled in unheated stations, sleeping on benches in grimy inns. My mother would not, of course, let us out of her sight. We would just sit and wait for "the agent." Doubtless, along the way there was an unseen agent or agents who directed operations for the thousands of immigrants who

shared our fate, but they did not share our particular journey. For I do not remember any groups of people who were bound in our direction. And until we got to Dresden we did not know that we were to sail from one of the German ports, perhaps Bremen, perhaps Hamburg.

At the Dresden station the mythical agent turned up. We were standing on the platform, a mother, not five feet tall, and five small children bewildered by passengers coming off the train and others rushing for it, when a face (now a blur) under a derby hat called my mother's name and ushered us into the station. It was an immense rotunda, the ceiling of multicolored glass, very beautiful, I thought. We were going to Rotterdam on a late train that night. Rotterdam? I knew it was a city in Holland. "But why?" asked my mother. Other people were going to Hamburg, mostly to Hamburg or Bremen. Well, we would sail from Rotterdam. That's how it must be. He couldn't give any reasons. He would see that we were put safely aboard the train, and there would be someone to meet us at Rotterdam. We waited in the station. I remember vaguely that a woman, probably from whatever agency had our destiny in hand, bought us some supper, sausage, bread, apples, and tea. How I wanted to walk around the station; even to go outside. This was such a different world from rural Russia, language, dress, manners, the space, even the light—everything! But my mother wouldn't take her eyes off us. We sat rooted to the benches until the train came. The agent turned up and pushed us through the crowds on the platform and onto the train. And all I would remember of Dresden was the spacious station, the beautiful ceiling, the hubbub of an unfamiliar language.

The third-class trains in Europe of that day were well known for their inconvenience: lack of ventilation, lack of toilet facilities, overcrowding. It was late in the fall, and chilly, but the cars were unheated. The country was flat; the fields sere. The towns looked neat and would have been interesting, I knew, had I been able to explore them. We stopped at stations just long enough to get boiling water for our teakettle. In the compartment we made and ate the food we carried: bread, cracklings, pickles, [dried] apples, prunes.

Our fellow passengers were poor-looking folk, the men in cheap, faded suits and cloth caps; the women, though some wore colorful peasant dress, mostly wore shabby homespun. These appeared to be workers, perhaps going to jobs in industry, or field hands returning at the end of the season. Most spoke German, some Dutch, and now and then Polish. I heard no Russian, or Yiddish. And while some German is understandable to the Yiddish speaker, Yiddish is hardly understandable to Germans. So there was little conversation. And we seemed to be the only Russian-Jewish family going to Rotterdam at this time.

It was wet and cold in Rotterdam. We were put up in a cheap hotel near the harbor and told that our boat would be along in a day or

two. I do not remember how long we waited. One day was like another. My mother adhered rigidly to her refusal to let us leave her sight. One could not blame her; we were strangers with no language. . . . We could get lost. . . . And so Rotterdam, like other places, is a blur: low roofs and windmills in the distance, a low horizon, gray skies. And then we were taken aboard a small steamer and for two excruciating days and nights we churned across the rough North Sea. There were

few passengers, and none with whom we could communicate. I could make nothing of the Dutch language: the little German that I knew was of no help. But the boat bustled with the activity of the crew. The captain shouted orders. Some of the men sang.

We were unloaded on a grimy, slippery dock at Glasgow under a sky that was like lead. It drizzled. Although it was mid-afternoon, the gas jets flickered around the dock throwing shadows over casks and bales and figures glistening with moisture. We were met by an agent. (The introduction was always: "I'm the agent," and we trusted him implicitly.) He spoke in English to a young man in a high celluloid

Rotterdam 1900 / Nov.

Glasgow 1900

collar, and for the first time I heard the language I was to adopt and love. To my mother he spoke in Yiddish. We were taken to a hotel, an old, weather-beaten three-story building on the Clydeside. We had a room to ourselves with hard beds and unwashed windows looking out on the river which seemed crowded with craft; the greasy water lapping their sides looked like bilge.

I think we waited there two or three days for our boat to New York. The drizzle continued; there wasn't a glimmer of sun. The yellow, unshaded gas jet flickered and hissed like an angry bee. We had never seen this kind of light before. There was a tiny gas grate, but it was cold. It was so cold, we decided to go to bed to keep warm, and my mother blew out the light (as she would have a candle or kerosene lamp at home). Sometime later a pounding on our door awakened me. A man was shouting outside the door. I tried to wake my mother, but she didn't seem to hear. I shook her and shook her, and she groggily climbed out of bed, while I shook the other children awake, and the man continued to shout. My mother unlocked the door. The smell of gas was strong! The man rushed in and turned it off. Our first night in Glasgow we were nearly asphyxiated, and would have been if not for the chance passing in the hallway of another immigrant. We all learned that night that you turn gas lights off, and do not blow them out.

Days of terrible food, peering out the grimy window, and shivering in our room, and then another agent helped us board the *State of Nebraska*, our New York–bound ship. We were, of course, steerage pas-

sengers assigned to small stuffy cabins below deck. There were four bunks, one atop another. The small space around them was crowded with our baggage. All the passengers were fed in a common dining room, which was long, narrow, and dingy. The badly cooked

food and the constant pitching and rolling in that low-ceilinged room made dining a distressing affair. Thin stews, potatoes, herring, watery prunes were our unvarying fare, washed down with tea, weak cocoa, or thin canned milk.

The weather was bad. It stormed most of the time. The lower deck was swept by water. Most of the passengers were seasick and stayed in their bunks. Only rarely could the children stay on deck for more than half an hour.

Twelve days out of Glasgow we hit the worst storm of all. That night was one of utter desolation and despair. There was a rumor that the ship was foundering. At the supper table people looked at each other mutely, seeking something in one another's faces. My mother and youngest brother, Samuel, who suffered more than any of us from seasickness, were too ill to come to the dining room. The stewardess

helped me to the table with the three younger ones. The dining room rolled; dishes clattered and broke; food was spilled. The children cried. Then the lights went out. The attendants lit some lanterns to take us to our cabins. The winds were violent, and the mountainous waves terrified us. The lashing storm did not abate during the entire 19 days. The ship was driven off her course. The decks were constantly awash and now deserted except by the crewmen who waded up to their knees going back and forth bareheaded, faces sweating, calling to each other "pumps! pumps! pumps!"

But others were coming out of the cabins, making their way to the dining room, my mother and brother among them. A friendly

passenger told us that all passengers were ordered out of their cabins, and we reassembled in the dining room. There were stacks of life belts, and we were instructed in how to put them on. Then the sobbing and the weeping and the wailing began. Men and women were on their knees praying. Jews do not kneel at prayer, so my mother sat on the floor, weeping and supplicating God, and we sat around her terrified and quietly crying. It was an assembly of doom: cold, terror-stricken, helpless, yet clutching the hope that morning might bring relief. There was just one tiny light in a lantern that swung violently from side to side. And the people were like shadows too. Only they were wailing, crying, sobbing shadows. At daybreak the storm did subside some, and we were told to return to our cabins. The rolling was worse below, and it was more lonely, but there was reassurance that the boat was not going down. In the late morning I was able to make my way along the deck to the kitchen and bring back a kettle of hot water for our tea. The passengers had little desire for food that day. Most of them did not leave their cabins. They shared some of their food with each other: dried apples, prunes, figs. The ship still rolled violently, but the danger was past. And in two days more we saw Sandy Hook. Nineteen days of misery and terror were behind us.

Badly damaged, the ship limped into New York harbor. It was December 24, 1900. A stream of immigrants passed before the two medical examiners, one on either side of the flow of men, women, and children. We were in line, my mother and the five of us in front of her, the youngest, my little sister, first. The man in the white coat turned our heads toward his, pulled up our eyelids, and waved us on. It took scarcely half a minute for each. Years later when I learned more about trachoma, the dread eye disease for which immigrants were being examined, I wondered how those doctors, working at such speed, could really check it.

We were transferred from the ship to a launch and landed at Ellis Island. The day was warm, and I marveled at such winter weather. I thought of the deep snows of the Ukraine and wondered if New York weather was always so balmy. I was to know later that this was a rare winter day, Christmas 1900.

The large reception room was crowded. There was a babel of voices: I could recognize Yiddish, Polish, Russian; others were unfamiliar. Immigrant aid workers were calling out names. New arrivals rushed into the arms of waiting relatives. There were shrieks of greeting and sobs and faces wet with tears. My father was not among these.

My mother spoke to someone in Yiddish, and he led her to a desk where messages were received and taken. No, there was no word from my father. My mother was frantic. The agent had assured her that my father was informed of the date of our sailing and the name of our ship. He was expected to meet us. The clerk sent a telegram which it was hoped would reach him in time to take us off that day. We waited all day amid the hubbub of scores of milling people. There were many others waiting, sitting on the hard benches, children and bundles beside them. There was talk and complaints and grieving in various tongues and the intermittent relief of reunions, embraces, and tears of joy.

There was no reply to the telegram, and my father did not come. The day went, and the waiting room emptied out; the clerks were leaving their desks, and the night attendants were making arrangements for lodging the unclaimed immigrants. We were put in a large dormitory with several rows of bunks, reserved for women and children. My mother was in a state of despair, as were many others whose husbands, sons, fathers, or other kin failed to take them off. I still hear the plaintive aria of one Italian woman, who seemed to pour out her heart in her musical voice, to the accompaniment of sighs and sobs.

We were awakened early, and there was some kind of a meal that few seemed to want. Once again we were in the waiting room, and at the gate leading into it were already anxious faces of waiting relatives. "Here he is! Here he is!" my mother cried out, and my father was waving excitedly. Soon he was admitted to the waiting room, and we surrounded him. He wept. And soon, after some details about release papers, baggage, etc., we were ferried across to a landing and the elevated line.

The train ran along close to grimy buildings with iron fire-escapes festooned with clothes and bedding. The day was unusually warm for December. Some of the windows were raised, and curtains fluttered in the breeze. Could these be dwellings? I had some naive ideas about American cities: wide streets, white houses, trees. (I was to know such later.) But my introduction to New York was a shock. The shock

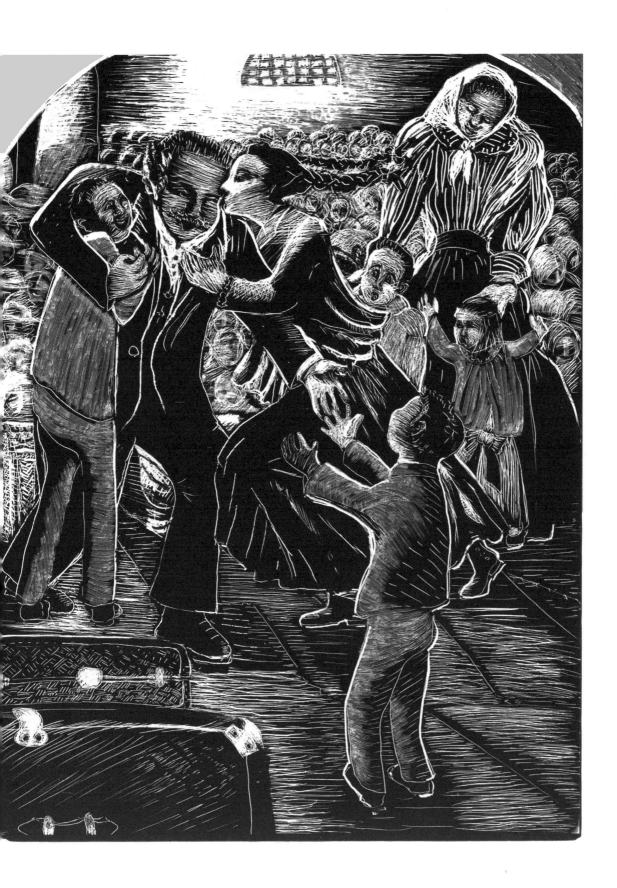

continued as we dismounted from the elevated and walked along the crowded, noisy, smelly streets to the tenement building at the corner of Orchard and Rivington Streets. We were jostled along by peddlers with pushcarts, women with shopping bags. Immigrants were a familiar sight, and they paid us scant attention. But the children did ogle us and called out, "Greenhorns! Greenhorns!" They knew us by our clothes and our bundles.

Our cold-water flat on Orchard Street was five flights up. It had four rooms, but only the front room facing the street and the kitchen facing a barren courtyard had windows. The two inner rooms, to be used as bedrooms, had only transoms over the doors leading into the other rooms. The toilet adjoined the kitchen. There was neither bath nor washbowl. During the seven months we lived there we washed in the kitchen sink and took our baths in a galvanized tin washtub. My father had put in the minimum necessary furnishings: beds, a table and four chairs in the kitchen, which also served as the dining room; the stove, I think, was furnished by the landlord. The living room had a little square oak table and two oak chairs with imitation leather seats and a rocker to match. There were white "lace" curtains on the two windows. Two gas jets inside glass shades were suspended from the ceiling. All these things he had to get on payments of a dollar a week.

The living room and kitchen seemed pleasant enough; the bedrooms with just light filtering through the transoms were dark. There were no clothes closets, only pegs along one wall in each and on the doors. My mother fixed a clothes line across and put up calico curtains over our clothes, as she had done in Russia. All the floors were bare. And although the winter was a mild one, we were never warm enough. Coal for the kitchen stove was brought up at a quarter a sack; wood the same. There was no room for more than a couple of sacks and rarely money to buy more than that. In the living room we had a portable kerosene heater, which was carried from one spot to another and gave off more fumes than heat.

My father had lost his job a month or so before our arrival. We had been scheduled by the agent to arrive just about that time. In addition to his worry about a job, he had been frantic with concern over our safety, for the agent had assured him that we would be leaving from either Hamburg or Bremen, he wasn't sure which, but there was no cause for worry, he had been assured.

He was completely bewildered when he heard how we traveled—to

Rotterdam, to Glasgow. And when he found that we had come on the *State of Nebraska* he blanched and trembled. The ship had been reported missing, or lost. It was never explained why we were routed as we were: halfway across Europe, up to the North Sea and across to Scotland, and the longest route across the Atlantic. No immigrant I had ever met from the Ukraine to the United States was ever routed that way.

MATILDA WROTE THIS STORY MANY DECADES AFTER the events, but many details are fresh—the long summer, the preparations for traveling, waiting to leave instead of continuing with her education that fall. She had wanted to go on to gymnasium, the equivalent of high school, but immigration cut short her education.

Fear of persecution and lack of employment urged flight, and though her family lived in the most food-secure part of the Russian Empire, Matilda describes simple food and periods of scarcity. Preserving food for the winter was usual, so her mother prepared for travel as she might have prepared for winter. Dried meat and fruit were packed to supplement the family's fare for this journey. Tea was essential. Among the few household items the family carried was a samovar, passed down to me. She always said that she was sorry that her mother bought a new one for America, because Matilda thought the one left behind more beautiful. I treasure the one that made the journey. It remains to me an emblem of Matilda.

Her account of the terrifying journey out of czarist Russia to America is vivid. Although the route the family took across Europe, from Galicia and finally to Glasgow, is a blur, she gives us moments of acute perception—the dirty, uncomfortable trains, the splendor of the Dresden railway station. In 1900, that magnificent structure must have been an enchantment for a girl from a small provincial town so far from the capitals of Europe, a girl who had never seen a train until she boarded that first one at the Romanian border.

Bertha, Matilda's mother, ignorant, illiterate, and monolingual, was under enormous pressure, worried about her five children, numbly following the instructions of the ubiquitous agents who, like today's "coyotes" that conduct people from Mexico and Central America through the desert and across the border to America, guided the family for a fee, turning up at the end of each leg of the journey. She had little knowledge of geography, as her daughter tartly reports, and although Matilda certainly had a better grasp after seven years of diligent scholarship in her town school, she was only thirteen. Her acute memory creates clear images of the journey and its terrors, especially her description of the horrific Atlantic crossing.

Because Matilda supplies the name of the ship and the date of the family's arrival in New York, I was able to locate a copy of the ship's manifest and a photo of the boat they boarded. I could easily imagine the panic of being trapped in the middle of the Atlantic on a ship—an unseaworthy vessel that nearly foundered and was reported lost. Information I found about the craft revealed how truly perilous the journey was. The *State of Nebraska* was decommissioned the year following the family's arrival. It carried just over one thousand passengers, and more than eight hundred of them traveled steerage. Matilda doesn't dwell on this, but the noise, the stench, and the unsanitary conditions must have been unbearable. She and her family, and hundreds of thousands of others over the years, bore them and survived.

Reading through the ship's manifest raises more questions. Matilda's mother's name, listed first, as "Braire," must be a misspelling. Perhaps it was Breine, a name a Jewish girl might have had and similar to Reina, also not uncommon. In America she was known as Bertha. Her age is given as thirty-four, and the ages of all the children that follow make them two years younger than they actually were. Was this an effort to avoid paying full fare for all of them, or just another mistake by the person hurriedly filling out the manifest? "Mary," who was always called Minnie but was no doubt named "Miriam," is listed as two years old. Since their father had been gone for five years, it's hardly possible, as Bertha was certainly a faithful wife, if not a happy one. Perhaps a two-year-old traveled gratis, and a five-year-old would have been charged at half fare. "Saloman" [sic] became Sam, "Moses" was Morris in America, "David" remained David, but the biggest surprise of all is Matilda's name as it appears on the manifest: "Taube." She always told us that she was originally named Tanya.

Among Matilda's papers are two short stories about the crossing, one typed, and titled "A Christmas Story for my Grandchildren." Another is written in longhand and is untitled. "A Christmas Story for my Grandchildren" was written in 1951, and I don't remember reading it then, but some of it was familiar on rereading. Intended for me and my brothers, it ends thus: "and as you have probably guessed by now, the little girl, Tanya, was your grandmother." The Ukrainians, Russians, and Poles she lived among may have called her by the Russian name, and it may have been how she was known at school, but the family knew her as "Taube," meaning "dove" in German or Yiddish. So strong was the impression of that journey that she wrote a third story, a fictionalized account of the experience that gives the main character's name as Manka, but in the manuscript, underneath a row of typed x's, I made out another discarded name—"Taube." Other names she tried were "La Paloma" ("dove" in Spanish) and Reina, like her mother's name—all struck out with an x. Taube sometimes becomes "Toby" in the new world, and Taube sounds like Tovah, meaning "good" in Hebrew. Why was the original name so completely lost until I recently discovered it? Did she reject it as just too shtetl-Jewish? Did it have too many painful associations, or was it just too mild and stereotypically feminine for Matilda's forceful personality?

The May Laws of 1882, enacted scarcely five years before Matilda's birth, and the addenda enacted in following years, possibly hold a clue. Did she know or remember, when she tells us that she may have entered school some time before she was eligible, that a law had been passed in 1893 that forbade Jews to adopt Christian names? She entered school around the time this law was passed. Did she tightly embrace her Russian name and bury the Yiddish one as an act of revolt? "Matilda," her American name, a name neither Jewish nor Slavic, possibly was adopted in rebellion—its meaning, "maid of battle," so appropriate.

She doesn't mention an aunt who, according to the manifest, sailed with them, but I find Eidel Rabinowicz, age twenty-two, a few lines above the rest of the family's entries. Matilda says that her father was orphaned at a young age and reared by his aunt. He didn't have a sister. She never speaks of any aunts on the paternal side, although she describes her mother's sisters and brothers who later joined the family in this country. For her destination, Eidel provides the address of Matilda's father (who is listed as "Itzik," not Yaakov, or Jacob, his actual name), 107 Rivington Avenue. Was Eidel a fellow passenger, one of the few Jews on board, also traveling without papers, someone that Bertha befriended and suggested she become her sister-in-law for immigration purposes? Acquiring relatives in this fashion may not have been uncommon.

3 THE WRETCHED REFUSE OF YOUR
TEEMING SHORES

The winter, fortunately, continued mild. I remembered the deep snows and the frozen river at Litin; the long wait for the loosening up of the frozen earth; the cruelty of extreme cold. Fortunate, indeed, for we had little adequate clothing to meet outdoor winter needs even in a less severe season. And walking the mile and a half to my first job in a shirtwaist factory on Walker Street in the early morning was far from comfortable.

I became 14 in the new century—January 9, 1901, just two weeks after arrival. My father wanted us all to be entered at school at once. But I was reluctant. Perhaps from recognition that as the eldest I should begin at once to earn something, since my father earned very little in odd jobs he was able to get; perhaps partly from the shock of disappointment with the ugliness and the poverty of New York as I beheld it. Friends talked of night school, and I decided to try it for the time being. The younger children were all entered at the nearest school. I found a job, clipping threads off the finished shirtwaists at two-and-a-half dollars a week. I worked a ten-hour day and half a day on Saturday. I carried a roll with a slice of meat or cheese in it and an apple for lunch and some sweetened thin coffee in a tin container that could be warmed on a gas plate. We had half-hour lunch breaks and quit work at half past five.

The thread clipping was tedious. But the place was warm, and there was the promise of later becoming a machine operator with an increase in wages. There were many young girls who clipped threads—trimmers we were called. Only two or three were as little as I was. Since I didn't have the necessary working papers, when a factory inspector was expected the forelady would tell me to get into a big packing case, at her signal, and to sit on the bottom of it covered lightly with a shirtwaist until he passed.

The sweatshop industry flourished. Thousands upon thousands of immigrants arrived and remained in New York. The needle trades were a catchall for young and old. The Jews were running away from the pogroms, the Italians from starvation, and these two groups formed the largest working force in the burgeoning clothing industry. In thousands of tenements, cellars, dingy stores, and decayed lofts in firetrap buildings, men, women, and children worked day and night. In bad light, in foul air, they cut and stitched and pressed and packed and dragged bundles and boxes and pushcarts and broken-down baby carriages through New York's East Side streets. Competition was savage. Jobs were contracted at the lowest possible bids, then sub-contracted and sub-subcontracted and spread out among women and children, whole families working together to keep from starving.

Neckwear was one of the sweated products that lent itself especially for homework. The article was small and light, and dozens could be carried in a pasteboard box. Children even could bring and deliver several gross of neckties. And children could turn and fold seams while mothers pressed and counted dozen after dozen into gross after gross.

My mother got some of this work. These were string ties, of some glossy mixed material—mostly cotton. They came to her just stitched on the inside. With a long flat rod, pronged at the end, a long strip of lining was pushed into the tie, which was turned at the same time. Then the seam was creased; the children could do this. Then the ties were pressed, tied into dozens, then twelve dozen into a gross, and a dollar was earned. One dollar for turning, creasing, pressing, and bundling 144 string ties, just about one-half cent apiece. But a dollar a day, seven dollars a week earned at home, my two and a half a week, and my younger brother's two dollars earned after school as an errand boy for an insurance office was almost half our income; my father's earnings were little more than that.

At various times after my mother joined

my father in this country, she tried to get some little business going: a little grocery, a little candy store. But these ventures failed as soon as they got started. My father just wasn't interested. After a long day's work at the Yale & Towne lock plant, or the Locomobile factory, he preferred to sit with his paper and a glass of tea, to visit with friends. He was very unhappy with my mother, but he bore her constant nagging with infinite patience. He loved his children. I have no recollection of his ever punishing us. He just begged us to do better. And he grieved over any harshness in his own conduct. How little I understood or appreciated this gentle, humble soul! I remember one bitter cold night, when he stood at the window and watched the raging blizzard and worried about my two younger brothers who were out selling newspapers. They were late coming home. When they finally came in numb with cold, feet half frozen, my father pulled off their wet coats, shoes, and socks. Sobbing he rubbed them to warmth as his hot tears fell on their chilled feet.

I was laid off with the spring slack season, soon after I became a machine learner. I did not look for another job, but worked with my

mother on the neckties. I did not like night school. There were mostly older people there and little appeal in the teaching of the language. The girls in the tenement of my own age went to day school, of course, and had their companions on the steps or walked together on the sidewalk. I could not speak their language, and although I listened seriously to their use of it, I remember learning very little English during our sojourn in the Orchard Street tenement. The little I did learn I spoke very guardedly, being conscious with childish pride of how well I commanded the Russian language and resentful of being inferior. My complete infatuation with English did not come until much later.

The shock of disappointment with the city that I had pictured in my childish imagination so completely differently doubtless created a sense of alienation, a feeling of not belonging that remained with me always about New York. I came and went to and from the city in later years in various circumstances—lived there off and on, commuted there from Connecticut—but I never was at home there, never belonged.

The six months that we lived in the Orchard Street flat were not, however, without interest. The streets surged with anxious, struggling humanity. The pushcart peddler was everywhere. From morning to evening and into the night one heard a constant medley of their raucous calls. Women with shopping bags pushed among the vendors pawing fish, vegetables, fruit; bargaining, contesting weights and measures, meeting offense with offense, giving as good as they got. These were poor people. Every penny was hard-earned and had to be watched. There was intense competition among the dealers and abuse, and often violent quarrels. To the newcomer nothing like this was known in the old world. Pious old Jews were shocked at the blasphemy they heard, and gentle Jewish grandmothers sighed at the ill-mannered new generation. But such undertones went unnoticed and were lost in the din and crush of the struggle for existence.

As the days grew warmer more children were on the street, playing hopscotch and dancing on the sidewalks. The Italian hurdy-gurdy

and the red-capped monkey became a familiar sight. In the evening older girls and boys would be seen standing in the doorways and on steps, or walking about. They would buy roasted chestnuts and sweet potatoes, peanuts from smoking little carts lighted with small acetylene flares. All this interested me, but I had no way of participating in it. If I had gone to day school I might have found girls of my own age to walk with and talk to. But since the only time I ever saw them was on the steps, I was reticent to talk to them, fearing they would laugh at my struggling English. So I stayed at home without young friends and tried to do what I could with the readers the younger children brought from school.

There was nothing near that suggested spring growth: no trees, no flowers, no grass, only the streets, the sidewalks, the stoops of the tenements. Now and then a pushcart vendor would have small pots of geraniums. These were a luxury at a quarter each, and I looked longingly but never bought one. Years later in California, where the geranium is considered a weed, I often thought of my youthful yearning for pots of geraniums on the window sill, and weed or not, I always have loved the flower.

My father's employment continued poor, and there was less and less work for Mother and me on the neckties as the summer drew near. One of our friends, a metalworker, had gotten work in the Yale & Towne lock factory in Stamford, and Father decided to try for a job there also. We had never been more than a few blocks away from our tenement, and this was an exciting prospect. We moved there in June.

With our few sticks of furniture and personal baggage we boarded a quaint little steamboat, the *Shady Side*, at a slip on the East River and chugged into the Long Island Sound. Down the years I have remembered the exhilaration we felt as we left New York behind.

What a contrast to our surreptitious flight from the Ukraine! The air was fresh; the water sparkled and churned gently against the boat. Sometimes the shoreline was near enough to glimpse trees and green terraces. The sky was open and blue—a lovely early June day. I was

thrilled. This—this is what I wanted! Perhaps we were approaching a place beyond the congestion and grime, the human jungle of New York. Four happy, dreamy hours were brought to an abrupt end as the *Shady Side* bumped to a stop against a splintery little dock. We walked down the gangplank led by father, onto a dirt road, rutted and muddy. But ahead was drier ground, and a path led across a field strewn with buttercups and daisies, and in the midst of the field a profusely blooming bush I recognized at once—a lilac bush! Rushing forward, I threw my arms around it and held the blooms to my face. Tears slid down my cheeks. My father must have felt my agitation. He turned away, perhaps to hide his own emotions, for he was also sensitive and easily moved.

We occupied the upper part of a two-story frame house, owned by a blacksmith, who had his forge and horseshoeing shed a few doors away. Our rent was six dollars a month. There were four light rooms and a back porch overhanging a mud-baked backyard, shared by the family downstairs. But there was some space for the children to play in. And there was an adjoining lot where my brothers soon took to the American game of baseball.

My father's wage was a dollar and a half a day, a ten-hour day. The old firm of Yale & Towne, founded in 1868, was the principal and nearly the only industry in Stamford. It employed several thousand workers and was notorious for low wages and unyielding open-shop policy. Skilled mechanics with years of service were getting two dollars a day. Young women got a dollar a day. The company was

supreme in its domination, not only of its workers, but of the town as well. It kept out all other industries for nearly half a century and then permitted only some small and uncompetitive ones to enter. And it was not until 1945, and after a bitter strike lasting three months, that the Congress of Industrial Organizations was able to get a foothold there—three-quarters of a century of complete domination by the Yale & Towne dynasty.

Even with a six-dollar-a-month rent and bread at ten cents a loaf, my father's wage could not maintain the family. Soon, my two brothers, ten and twelve years old, were selling newspapers, and the third one, two years younger, followed shortly. My mother washed and scrubbed and made some of our clothes on an ancient sewing machine. A year after our arrival in the country she bore another son. And less than two years after, still another and the last. She was extremely frugal—what else could one be on such income? A good housekeeper and fearful of debt, she loved her children, of course, but she was harsh, while my father was both devoted to us and gentle. Their life together to the very end was unhappy.

That first summer in Stamford was lovely. There was open sky and trees and the Long Island Sound within walking distance. I picked up quite a bit of English. In the fall I went to school! By Thanksgiving I could read

The Landing of the Pilgrims fairly fluently with one glaring error. Reading aloud, I pronounced the word "dessert" instead of the word that was written, "desert," bringing a roar of laughter from the class and causing me to turn scarlet with shame.

I think I started the year in the sixth grade. I made rapid progress, once I acquired enough language. In the other major subjects, arithmetic and geography, I was in advance, having had the equivalent of elementary schooling in Russia. At the end of the school year I had completed the eighth grade and was graduated. My parents said nothing about my going on to high school. It was expected that I go to work.

Now it was summer again and I was 15. There was no industry for women in Stamford then. Some women worked in the Yale & Towne factory, but I was too young, really just too little, to be acceptable there. I could sew and had a flair for trimming hats. A neighbor thought I would make a good milliner. Why not try it? So I became an

apprentice in one of the two small millinery stores in town. I was paid three dollars a week. The hours were from eight to six, half day on Saturday. In six months I learned the trade thoroughly, but there was no job for me. None of the other three workers were leaving; there was no place either in the other store. So I had a trade, but no place to ply it, except of course in New York where the industry was flourishing.

The thought of going to New York upset me a great deal, but eventually the decision was made. There was no alternative. I was now 16 and I had a trade, a distant relative of father's would board me, and New York was only 30 miles from Stamford. I found a job in a millinery factory easily enough, for the season was on. The rates were for piecework, and I could make about six dollars a week, but it was no longer a craft. At long tables sat 50 or more copyists. The same model was copied over and over again; the same operation was repeated by all, until the model was replaced by another, and the same process continued—very different from my knowing and doing everything on one hat for one or two, or perhaps no more than six, customers. No longer an artisan, I hated the mass production.

At the end of the season I came home, and I never resumed the trade. I worked for a time as a clerk in a grocery store and in a dry goods store. When a small shirtwaist factory came to town I became quite a skilled machine hand. There were periodic slack seasons, mostly during spring and summer. Once during a protracted layoff, I went to New York and got a job as a clerk in Hearn's Department Store on 14th Street. The pay was $11 every two weeks and one-percent commission on sales. I was selling table linens and would sometimes make as much as three dollars a week in commissions. I lived in Brooklyn with the distant relative, paid five dollars a week for room and board, and walked across the bridge to save carfare, then paid a nickel to get to the store. I think I worked there for about four months. The summer brought me back home. Summers always made the city unbearable for me, the heat, the stench, the oppressiveness of grinding poverty that surrounded me, and the absence of any vegetation. Even years later

I gave up what were considered good opportunities to get away from New York.

I think that the five years spent in Stamford were the most tranquil. We were poor, but even though our housing and general living conditions were inferior, our family had friends close by and their daughters were my friends. I was especially close to two of them. And there was Nathan, my first beau.

He was two years older and a machinist's apprentice. He early became a Labor (Socialist) Zionist and was studious and earnest. He read a lot in both English and Yiddish and had generally cultivated tastes. We used to read together, take long walks, and go to the theater when there was a stock company in town. My father was very fond of him and would often engage him in Hebrew commentary. He would have liked him as a son-in-law. I was not much in love with him though, and when we moved to Bridgeport and he went to New York, our romance came to an end.

We moved to Bridgeport when my father got a job as a mechanic in the Locomobile factory. I think the going wage then was three dollars a day. Father may have earned a little more. I went to work in Batcheller Brothers Corset Factory. This was the oldest of a number of old corset factories in Bridgeport, perhaps the oldest in Connecticut. The Thompson's Glove Fitting brand corset made there had quite a reputation.

Bridgeport was an ugly town in 1906, and it grew uglier with its rapid growth as an industrial town. During the First World War it was called "the Essen of America." There were, of course, fine residences and spacious lawns and lovely gardens (I once worked as a child's nurse in one of these), apart from the scarred, polluted, and disfigured industrial sections. But these refuges of opulence and tranquility were at some distance from both ends of the drawbridge that linked the sections of town that housed the industries and their workers. Working-class families clustered as close as possible to the factories, and most of them walked to work. Half hour's walk to the factory was considered ordinary. With twenty minutes one could go home for dinner at midday within the hour allowed. I did. And when I later rode a bicycle, I had ten minutes or so, time to spare for reading.

But the workers' homes were still mostly one- or two-family frame houses with backyards and front porches. The weathered paint, mostly brown or gray, always made them look shabby. Most of the streets were unpaved and muddy during rainy weather. But there were still trees along the sidewalks, and in the spring and summer little patches of gardens abounded. I liked our shabby little house with the kitchen and sitting room downstairs and three small bedrooms upstairs. I considered it a luxury to have a room to share with my sister. And for the first time I had a desk—a three by five pine table—which I fitted up with a large blotter, bookends, and pencil tray. I scrubbed the pine floor weekly and beat the small rug in front of the bed vigorously. There were white sash curtains at the windows. There was an old trunk covered with cretonne. I did not covet much more. My wants were then, and remained always, simple.

The corset factory where I worked was a long three-story brick building, overgrown with ivy. It employed probably 300 workers, mostly women, of course. I became an operator on a double-needle machine. I earned only five or six dollars a week while learning, but later was able to make $12 a week by piecework. The work week was 55 hours: a ten-hour day and half day on Saturday.

The workers were mostly native

Anglo-American stock with a goodly mixture of Irish Americans—
the older women. I was the only Eastern European immigrant. I heard
the Yankee twang, accents from the "Immoral Isle," now and then a
Scottish burr, but mostly it was the ordinary vernacular peppered
with slang. There was talk going on all the time. Once an operation
was mastered, it became entirely mechanical. Only the skill of fingers
and the guidance of the eye were necessary. So the women chattered.
Monday morning would bring a rash of accounts of what they did
on Saturday, on Sunday: the washing and ironing and cleaning and
marketing, the husbands' demands, the children's needs. Work, work,
work. But hope, too. Maybe one day they could stop going to the
factory. What couldn't they do at home then! None of these women
worked for "pin money"; their earnings were necessary to the family
survival.

The girls talked of other things: clothes (they made their own
mostly), beaux, the Saturday night dance, the hope of marriage and

quitting the job. And there were always the Sunday supplements with their vicarious thrills of romance and "society" scandals.

My own weekends were not different to any great extent. I had washing and ironing, too— my own. I made my own clothes, and if I didn't spend much time on Sunday papers, I had other reading to do. Only I couldn't talk about this kind of reading. Oh, I spoke English fluently enough by this time. If there was a trace of a foreign accent in my speech it was what my fellow workers chose to call "bookish." Doubtless it was, because I did turn to books for an education. My schooling ended when I was 15, and I did not see the inside of a classroom again until years later when I attended a summer extension course at Columbia University, but my thirst for knowledge continued in spite of the lack of formal education.

I would have liked to talk about the books I read, but one or two attempts convinced me that I was a bore. Well, I didn't have to talk, and I didn't have to think much about the continuous chain of corset gores running under the two needles and falling into a trench. So I thought about the books and remembered passages and recited poetry to myself.

I clearly remember my discovering the poetry of Ridgely Torrence during that time and one particular poem that I memorized. It began with the line, "I know what the caged bird feels, alas!" It expressed my mood during the spring, as the days grew longer and the skies bluer, and the trees began to bud. The job became very irksome, and somehow I felt better as I recited the lines and identified myself with the captive bird. Years later while watching the Howard University Players do one of Torrence's plays, that poem and that mood came back to me in poignant memory.

No, I didn't like making corsets, thousands and thousands and tens of thousands of pairs month in, month out. From time to time there was a layoff. That gave me more time to read, to sew—for myself and the family. When the layoffs at Batchellers' were over-extended I tried the other corset factories. There was Warner's and Birdseye-Sommers. I worked in both. It was in Warner's that I first faced the employment manager to ask for an increase in some of the piece rates. With two other girls as a committee and filled with fear, I haltingly stated our request. We were not asked to sit down. A cynical smile spread across the man's face; he screwed up his eyes, looked us up and down, and said, "You're pretty well dressed for girls

who are complaining about poor wages," and curtly dismissed us. Warner's was then considered the most modern corset factory in New England, and its American Lady model was a great success. It was also the largest and the most oppressive factory, with its modern efficiency. I went back to Batchellers'.

Two years after we moved to Bridgeport, my grandfather and his family, three sons and two daughters, came from Russia. My grandmother had died the year before. The eldest son, Isaac, had been married and divorced. He was in his late thirties. A slender, handsome man with a gentle disposition, he had done nothing in Litin, since he had no craft. In Bridgeport he found work in a metal factory at two dollars a day. He soon married and had three boys who were in their teens as handsome as their father. They all went into Bridgeport factories.

The second son, Aaron, was in his midthirties. He was the one who had eked out a few rubles a month by teaching peasants to read and write. He considered himself an intellectual and above factory work. He looked to marriage to a girl whose family might afford him a place in business as a way out of his employment dilemma. Since there always had been marriage brokers among the Jews in Europe, the profession had its counterpart in America. There were always marriageable daughters, old maids, as orthodoxy would have it, almost in their midtwenties. Indeed, after a brief search and with a smattering of English gained in night school Aaron married the daughter of a grocer, a plain but ambitious girl past thirty. Her father was well along in years, and the daughter had long managed the store. Now her husband joined the management. They had three children, a boy and two girls. I was no longer in Bridgeport when they were growing up, but years later I saw one of the girls, now about twenty, who had come to Los Angeles with her mother to try her fortune in Hollywood. She was a dancer, a pretty girl, completely dominated by her mother, who was madly ambitious for her daughter and as aggressive as I had remembered her.

My youngest uncle, Adam, and the youngest of the family, was 24 when they came. Although he was no less literate than his brother Aaron, he had no illusion about his status. He went to work in a wire-producing factory and soon lost two fingers off his left hand. When he was cheated out of compensation he gave up factory work in disgust. He became an electrician's helper, mastered the trade, and became a contractor. He married a woman older than himself, and they had a boy and a girl. Adam amassed something of a small fortune but was obsessed with the fear of losing his money. He would not keep it in any bank, but in secret hiding places. When he died suddenly, none of it could be found. The family owned the house, a poor little frame cottage. The walls and floors were torn up in search of the cache, but nothing was ever found.

Of my two aunts, the younger one, Rebecca, 26, was quite beautiful. Of medium height, slender, with lovely light brown hair, she was gentle and intelligent. Clara was four years older, and an old maid, alas! Both girls got jobs in a garment factory but were married within the year. And within another year Rebecca was dead of puerperal fever. The baby died six months later. Clara, easygoing and dull, married a widower with a small boy, and they went to live in Hartford. My grandfather, a sturdy old patriarch, lived out his years with one or another son. He was past 90 when he died.

THE FAMILY LIVED ON ORCHARD AND RIVINGTON FOR A very short time. While her descriptions of the Lower East Side sound similar to others I have read, and though Matilda expresses interest in the energy and life she observed in New York, I am struck by a grievance that recurs—the absence of greenery ("no trees, no flowers, no grass"). Throughout her story she is depressed in New York and longs to be in the countryside, especially in the summer. How deeply she felt the absence of any reminder of the natural world (except, of course, for the geraniums). The town where she grew up was surrounded by countryside. There was a river with trees and fields close by, and the lilacs she mentions in the churchyard next door to her grandparents' house. The town's proximity to nature may have been one of the few things Matilda missed. New York, with its lack of open space, crowding, and filth, must have been a stunning contrast. No wonder she was overcome with longing and nostalgia seeing the lilac bush at the top of the muddy path when the family landed at the dock in Stamford. This encounter echoes throughout the memoir in her vivid descriptions of nature, her thirst for beauty and longing for the fresh air and peaceful environment outside the city, especially as summer approached.

Her disclosure of the moment of embarrassment during her year of public school in Stamford contrasts with her school years in Litin where she was regularly insulted. The gales of laughter elicited by the mispronunciation of an English word seem slight compared to the daily abuse by the Slavonic teacher in the Pale, who hated Jews and punished Tanya (Taube) and her Jewish classmates for the smallest infractions. And learn she did! With no small pride, she reports that she finished three years in one in America, and she implies that the quality of the education she received in the town school in Russia, with all its bigotry, was superior to the one-year experience with American grammar school education. Her classmates called her "Tillie," but her American teacher, disapproving of nicknames, decided she would be "Matilda." And Matilda she remained.

Then at fifteen she went to work again, and she would continue to work until she collected her social security pension at the age of fifty-five.* A repeated theme in the memoir is a classic depiction of "the alienation of labor." For example, she learns a skill, millenary, only to find work on an assembly line in a sweatshop in New York City ("I hated the mass production," she writes). She explains how the dissatisfaction born of never being responsible for a complete "work" numbs and alienates the worker from her work. This was even more apparent in the later entries about Batcheller Brothers, the corset factory where she toiled in Bridgeport.

A photo discovered in the Reuther archives shows Matilda peeking out, with characteristically cocked head, a little, dark face, craning to be seen among all her taller Anglo-American workmates on the steps of the ivy-covered factory, the prettiest girls or the most powerful ones in front.

I remember now her refusal to wear any undergarments but panties and slips and wonder if her labor in the corset factory influenced

---

*She began accruing social security insurance when the program started in 1935. By that time she had been working for more than thirty years. And yet the monthly check, along with the small savings she accumulated, was sufficient to meet her needs. When she died, her assets totaled $400. Each of her grandchildren inherited $100.

her—the corset a metaphor for restriction and confinement. In the 1950s, she laughed at women with small breasts wearing a bra: "I have nothing to put IN a brassiere." She thought girdles were an unnecessary discomfort, vanity only giving way where stockings and garters were concerned. She never wore a garter belt, as my mother did, only stockings rolled in garters just below the knee, concealed by the longish skirts of the 1940s and 1950s. The story Matilda tells about the cynical manager's pointing out the workers' stylish couture in her very first attempt at gaining better wages for herself and her coworkers resonates. She was always well dressed, concerned with style and quality in the clothes she wore. She often observed that she made her own clothes, though I remember her only mending, not sewing a whole garment as my mother did. She shopped in secondhand stores in the 1950s, before our generation embraced "vintage" wear, and she only bought "on sale." She had such tiny feet that size 4½ shoes, the model size, fit perfectly, so she wore very stylish and expensive footwear at low cost. In spite of a general fetishization of tiny feet, few women really could fit into those sample shoes.

Bridgeport, the "Essen of America," was a center of heavy industry and, like the German city on the Ruhr, was known for the manufacture of weapons (the Remington arms factory where one of her brothers later worked and the Winchester rifle works) along with other industrial steel and iron works. As in its German counterpart, coal burning and steel manufacturing turned the atmosphere dense and dirty. That environment, along with the air pollution Matilda experienced in New York and later in Los Angeles, undoubtedly contributed to the asthma from which she perpetually suffered.

And the numbing factory work continued.

A positive result of the family's move to Bridgeport in 1906 was more expansive quarters. Now Matilda shared a room with only her sister. I briefly wondered about the five brothers that must have shared a room the same size. The detail she gives about the room's décor indicates Matilda's pleasure with the arrangement and hints at an almost bourgeois sense of beauty and order. It also highlights her fondness for study. Her reading continued, unguided for the most part except for suggestions from David and fellow Socialists. It was odd to read her quote from the poem, so famous to my generation through Maya Angelou's memoir, *I Know Why the Caged Bird Sings.*

Matilda misattributes the poem to Ridgely Torrence, a lesser-known, white writer. The poem, "Sympathy," is actually by African American writer Paul Laurence Dunbar:

I know what the caged bird feels, alas!
    When the sun is bright on the upland slopes;
When the wind stirs soft through the springing grass,
And the river flows like a stream of glass;
    When the first bird sings and the first bud opes,
And the faint perfume from its chalice steals—
I know what the caged bird feels!

I know why the caged bird beats his wing
    Till its blood is red on the cruel bars;
For he must fly back to his perch and cling
When he fain would be on the bough a-swing;
    And a pain still throbs in the old, old scars
And they pulse again with a keener sting—
I know why he beats his wing!

I know why the caged bird sings, ah me,
    When his wing is bruised and his bosom sore,—
When he beats his bars and he would be free;
It is not a carol of joy or glee,
    But a prayer that he sends from his heart's deep core,
But a plea, that upward to Heaven he flings—
I know why the caged bird sings!*

*Poetry Foundation, https://www.poetryfoundation.org/poems-and-poets/poems/detail/46459.

I love the nineteenth-century addition: "alas." My Nana remembers the first line; Angelou remembers the last.

I wish she had provided more detail about her references to her parents' marital dissatisfaction. Was their unhappiness with each other a discouraging example? Did it have anything to do with her rejection of the tradition, making her wary of encumbering herself in what she later described to me as "a corrupt institution"? Certainly, she did not reject the idea of romantic love, as she tells us that she was "not much in love" with Nathan and thus ended her relationship with him. And without a notion of romance, her ten-year on-again, off-again relationship with my grandfather is inexplicable.

The women's suffrage movement in England was being discussed in the circles Matilda now traveled. The Industrial Workers of the World (IWW) was recently formed, and Matilda and her brother David were drawn to leftist politics and intellectual and artistic circles in Bridgeport. Both of them were reacting to the deadening factory work and exploitation they experienced from the time of their arrival in the United States. The Socialists and the syndicalists appealed to them. Besides meetings and lectures, they attended plays, where they heard the English of the elite, diction and accents that contrasted with the Scottish burr, Irish brogue, and Yankee twang so familiar from work. Works by Ibsen and Shaw were performed, along with the ubiquitous Shakespearean offerings and lesser-known playwrights of the day, like Susan Glaspell.

Jacob, Matilda's father, was working at the Locomobile factory in Bridgeport, before the advent of the assembly line. Locomobile was one of the most expensive American cars manufactured—one at a time by hand. The assembly line for automobiles would not develop for a couple of years, but the Model T had just been introduced, and General Motors recently had been founded in Detroit. Her maternal grandfather, Wolf, and his five adult children arrived in 1908, just a few years after the 1905 Revolution in Russia. The death of Matilda's grandmother, rather than the political situation, probably motivated the Schpanier family's immigration. And here they were, the "patri-arch" and all his children. Wolf Spanier [*sic*] is listed in the 1910 census at Matilda's parents' address in Bridgeport.

The death of her favorite aunt, just a few years older than Matilda, of puerperal fever, affected her deeply. Did she reflect on the dangers of childbirth when she decided, years later, to become a mother?

4   A NEW CAREER

About the time of the arrival of grandfather and family, there
arrived also a friend of my childhood in Litin. Leo was two
years older than I and had graduated from the Litin elementary
school ahead of me. When we left he was planning to go to the gymnasium in Kiev. When he came to this country six or seven years later
he set himself the goal of becoming a pharmacist. He worked as a
delivery boy and clerk in various drug stores and studied at night.
He finally got a job as an assistant in the pharmacy of the Montefiore
Home, then a hospital for chronic invalids. He visited us occasionally
in Bridgeport and talked about his progress. He was ambitious and
talked a great deal to me about his job and good standing at the hospital. He thought I ought to do better than to be a corset operator and
suggested that I get a job as a nurse there. The hospital had no regular
training school, but there was in-training for the specialized nursing
there. After my aunt's death, which had profoundly affected me, I
had taken a nursing course in the night school of the YWCA, and I
was in the mood to continue nursing. Leo urged me on. My parents
were agreeable to the idea. I was now 20, Leo was a childhood friend,
a promising young professional, and they hoped for a match.

I liked nursing at the home, though we had little instruction.
There were no regular classes, but in each ward a graduate nurse was
in charge, and under her supervision we nurse's aides learned as we

worked. We were started at $50 a month and maintenance, and after
a year the pay went up some and every year thereafter. The home was
far removed from the noise and congestion of the city, and that was
pleasant to me. Once a month or so, I had a long weekend and went
home to Bridgeport, which was 75 miles on the New York, New Haven
and Hartford Railroad. Usually Leo went with me, saving his free
time to coincide with mine. At the home it was generally assumed
that we were engaged, and indeed one weekend at my parents' home,
and at their behest, our engagement was formally announced among
our friends.

The nine or ten months that I spent at the home were perhaps the
most stable of any in my work experience. I read quite a lot. Among
the patients, mostly middle-aged and mostly Yiddish-speaking, there
was one, a paresis victim, who appeared to be well educated and who

liked to engage me in conversation. He read a great deal and liked to recite poetry and bits of eloquent political speeches. Lincoln was his idol, and I never heard the Gettysburg Address better spoken, nor the words "with charity toward all, with malice toward none" more profoundly impressive. It was through Mr. S, in fact, that I began to learn to appreciate the beauty of spoken English. The gratitude of the patients was a great satisfaction to me, and I thought seriously of continuing nursing as a profession. I planned to enter an accredited nurses' training school, and I filed an application at Mount Sinai Hospital.

This purpose, and indeed the course of my life, was abruptly changed by a scandal at the home. The elderly Hungarian woman in charge of supplies was discovered to have been pilfering the hospital bed linen. A long-time employee, she had appeared the model of efficiency and rectitude, and we were surprised that she was the culprit

and that she had been engaged in this underhanded activity for many years. Among those said to have been involved was Leo. He denied any part of it, but he was fired along with the Hungarian lady who had made something of a favorite of him. He left the home under a cloud, and I began to feel uncomfortable in the wake of the commotion and dismissals. Although reassured by the director that my own standing was in no way impaired, I became more and more restive and finally quit.

When I returned home, and after being away from Leo, I began to realize that I had no real affection for him. Our engagement had been a romantic episode based in childhood nostalgia and encouraged by the approval of my parents and by their fervent desire for my marriage to an ambitious professional and fellow landsman. His visits now irritated me. He pled his case ardently, enlisting the support of my parents. He was studying hard and working in a pharmacy and in another year would be so well established. . . . In spite of his entreaties and those of my parents I drew further and further away and during one of his visits declared our engagement off. He took it hard, and my parents took it even harder.

I had a few intermittent private nursing cases during the months following my return to Bridgeport. But nursing had lost its attraction. Soon I was working in the corset factory again. But now I was about to embark on another phase of my industrial and social experience.

LEO'S SUGGESTION THAT SHE COULD BETTER HERSELF by nursing and the death of her aunt seem to be the major motivators for Matilda's choice to embark on a new career. I find notable her singular compassion for the gentleman with what I assume to be "general paresis," which is specifically associated with syphilis, in contrast to "paresis," simple paralysis, at a time when venereal disease was not discussed in polite society. She expresses her admiration for his spoken English and his education, and she doesn't mention learning to make a bed with "hospital corners," the technique she taught me when I was very young, before the era of fitted sheets. I still make a bed with the hospital corner on the top sheet.

Matilda was clearly skeptical when Leo denied culpability in the linen theft, but the hospital blamed him as an accomplice, causing her to feel "restive." Obviously, the episode made her question the whole romance, and she called off the engagement. She doesn't really describe how it occurred or how Leo and her parents reacted, except that they "took it hard." Later she alludes to her estrangement from the family, but she always remained in contact with David and Bob, the first and last born of her brothers. And she was especially close to her sister, Minnie, who died early.

After Matilda's experiences, not only as a nurse, but also as a worker for the labor surveys, what motivated her return to the corset factory? Why had nursing "lost its attraction"?

Here her dissatisfaction with the path before her begins to appear. The course her family and society in general had laid out for her seemed more and more restrictive and unfulfilling; soon she would finally and resolutely turn away from filial duty and societal expectations.

5   BRIDGEPORT AND SOCIALISM

I was 22. My brother David was 20. He had also gone to work at 14, after graduating from elementary school. His jobs were mostly in small metal and appliance manufacturing factories, first in Stamford, then in Bridgeport, but for about two years before I returned from New York, he had a newspaper and magazine stand in the center of town and was the agent for several publications. The year was 1909.

Bridgeport was an industrial center with both light and heavy metal manufacturing. People were employed to fabricate building equipment, and the Locomobile automobile plant, where my father worked, was a big employer. The craft unions were relatively strong, and the Central Trades and Labor Council was the typically conservative, craft-minded body, seemingly unconcerned by the rapid development of mechanization. In politics it adhered to Samuel Gompers's well-known formula of rewarding friends and punishing enemies, always either Republican or Democrat. The council's two or three Socialists were of the mildest, what we called the post-office, type. Among them was Jasper McLevy, machinist, who later became mayor of Bridgeport and served many terms, remaining always the "post-office" or "municipal sewage plant" type. Among workers generally, though, the growing Socialist Party was making headway.

Out of our own frustrated dreams for an education, and the struggle of our family to make a living, my brother and I had become aware of economic conditions as they affected the working class. The need for us to go to work as young children made us conscious of general social and economic inequities. The trial of Charles Moyer and Bill Haywood affected me profoundly. The long drawn-out testimony reported in the press, the revelations of the struggle of the miners, the eloquence of Clarence Darrow, was the unfolding of labor's history and labor's struggle for me, and I followed every word, every nuance, with avidity. It opened my road to Socialism, never to be closed.

The Socialist Party was active on the Moyer-Haywood case with meetings and speakers and publicity. Its publications gave full play to the dramatic trial. My brother was caught up in the party's activities. He had become a member of the SP while I was still at the Montefiore Home, and I joined shortly after returning to Bridgeport.

The craft unions, typically, were cool toward the flourishing Socialist agitation that was spreading through the land. But if they were cool toward Socialism, they were hotly opposed to the industrial unionism which was carried on by the IWW and which gained many adherents among Socialists, and SP Local Bridgeport now had a faction advocating industrial unionism and urging commitment by the SP to its principle. This naturally led to much discussion and often to contention. The question was heatedly debated in every SP local. As some of the craft unionists were members of Local Bridgeport, the inevitable alignments took place. Those of the industrial unionism faction were called reds. The industrial unionists returned the compliment by calling the craft union adherents yellows. The fight between them grew and spread and became an issue in SP conventions. The official position on the SP was in favor of craft unions. The old, the staid, the politically conservative were represented there. The young, the vigorous, the radical element in the SP was industrial unionist.

When I returned to Bridgeport the fight was already going on in the SP local. It was easy for me to see the superior form and the pressing need for industrial unionism. The elimination of crafts, due to mechanization and specialization, was everywhere apparent. In the textile industry, in the garment industry, in scores of other industries, crafts as such simply did not exist anymore. Those who clung to small craft locals were impeding general organization among the workers. I never saw anyone make a whole corset, or half or a quarter of one. There were a score of operations, but each separate operation was repeated hundreds of times over by the same worker. And so it was in other industries.

Conditions in the corset factory were no different than they had been when I left to try nursing. There was still the 55-hour week and piecework. Now, though, I understood the need for organization. We could reduce our working hours. We could have something to say about pace and speed-up. At least we could do these things through a union. I talked to some of the girls, the younger ones. The older women were unapproachable, indifferent, but to my surprise neither

were the younger women very interested. They looked eventually toward marriage—marriage and freedom from the factory, or so they
thought. I persisted. But I was hardly popular.

I had no experience in organizing and I needed help. My appeal to
the Central Trades and Labor Council met with indifference. Perhaps
I could get some help from the Women's Trade Union League, which
was helping to organize women. Because I was a member, I wrote the
WTUL. The league sent down two organizers from New York, Le-
onora O'Reilly and Melinda Scott. We met, they gave instructions,
they helped to draw up a leaflet for distribution to my shop and left.
We were unsuccessful in getting up a meeting. Corset workers did not
become organized until long, long after.

But if the Central Trades and Labor Council was no help, neither
was the SP local. We talked about organization, we looked to an organized working class to support the SP, but we had no program and
no technique to help us in organizing unions. The SP left economic
organization entirely to the duly established and conservative craft

unions. It was concerned only with the political arm of the Socialist movement. How different is the history of the European Socialist movement! We tried, at any rate, to spread the acceptance of industrial unionism, at least. The *International Socialist Review* was its strongest advocate and the best and liveliest Socialist journal of that day. And we started a little sheet of our own called the *Industrial Unionist*.

The internecine quarrel continued both on a local and national scale. It led to a crisis. Locals split, members were expelled; Haywood was dropped as a member of the executive board of the SP. They were stormy years for the SP, which nevertheless reached its major growth during the time, only to rapidly decline with the beginning of World War I.

MATILDA RETURNED TO BRIDGEPORT AFTER THE Montefiore Home and went back to work in the corset factory. A broken engagement and abandoned nursing career brought her back to her parents' home. Limited options led to her need to resume factory work and her growing involvement with Socialism.

Searching for Matilda on the Internet under "Rabinowitz," I come across two articles she wrote under her original surname—digitized copies from a newspaper where she contributed an occasional column. The articles, about women and labor, accompany a column-wide photo of Matilda in shirtwaist and an enormous, wide-brimmed hat. Her deep-set eyes are dark and serious. She is twenty-two.

I studied the newspaper itself—the *Bridgeport Herald*, August 10, 1910. What kind of paper was this? As I scanned the ads and articles it became apparent that this was a Socialist-leaning paper—lots of announcements for Socialist lectures and other news about labor issues sympathetic to the workers. It surprised me that there were popular newspapers that had a left-wing editorial policy but operated like any capitalist paper, with advertising paying the bills along with subscriptions and newsstand sales. And the *Bridgeport Herald* wasn't any marginal left-wing newspaper. It was very widely read; its masthead bragged "the largest circulation in the state."

Headlines on the same page: in huge type, "Power and Influence of Socialism by Robert Hunter, Socialist Candidate for Governor"; an apparent editorial (now we call them "op-ed" pieces) about Bridgeport's growth and the debt the city owes to its wage earners for its position as second largest city in the state; finally, an illustrated "humor" piece on the hazards of wealth and advantages of poverty and obscurity (you won't get a bullet in your back).

Then, familiar to Matilda, no doubt, there were the want ads for corset factory jobs—Warner's and Batchellers' among them. On the page opposite a dozen ads for washing powder, for handymen, for purveyors of food—meat, butter, fish, and fresh pies—was this:

WANTED

Corset operators on lap seaming, gore making, stripping, flossing and other branches. Also hand workers, small girls. 100 new machines to be filled at once. Apply to The Warner Bros. Co. Lafayette and Atlantic Sts.

There is everything in this newspaper to attract wide readership: divorces, scandals, miscegenation, corrupt public officials, grisly crimes. Nearly everyone with a penny must have bought it.

Matilda didn't keep clippings of these opinion pieces written for the *Bridgeport Herald*; in fact there are no clippings that I can find among her papers, or in the archive, with one exception. Among the scant ephemera in her file is a clipping with no date, but probably from the 1940s: a photo of one of her brothers receiving a medal—the

Purple Heart. Private Morris Rabinowitz, a very small man, stands at military attention while two tall, pale men in uniform pin the honor on his breast. The caption says he was wounded in action during the Meuse-Argonne offensive in 1918. It is strange to see that Matilda, who abhorred war and the military, kept such a memento—but he was her younger brother. Perhaps she was proud of the bravery that awarding the Purple Heart confirms.

As my grandmother and her brother David longed for an education and struggled for workplace justice and fair wages, many workers were radicalized by thwarted aspirations for education, by exploitation as child workers, and by a desire for social and economic justice.

"I never saw anyone make a whole corset," Matilda declared. Mechanization and industrialization create alienation of labor, according to Marx. The dehumanization of industrial production was not only a preoccupation of the left. The burgeoning Arts and Crafts Movement lamented the spiritual toll mass production extracted, not only for the worker, but also for the consumer of industrial goods. The American intelligentsia that adopted the views of British thinkers John Ruskin and William Morris believed that beauty was as necessary to life as bread, and these ideas were reflected in the Lawrence strike's slogan "Give us bread, and give us roses, too." These ideas influenced Matilda. A beautiful and harmonious home and simple, good-quality furnishings were always sought, almost always purchased on sale or secondhand. Her thirst for beauty was evident in the domestic spaces she created and the few, handsome, simple utilitarian objects she acquired.

Matilda admired craftsmanship and the artisans that practiced it. The Locomobile factory where her father worked produced cars by hand. I was surprised to find that, in spite of their funny name, these automobiles were very desirable and expensive, affordable only to elites.

She describes her brother David's involvement with the Socialist Party and her close following of the Haywood-Moyer trial. Three leaders of the Western Federation of Miners, Bill Haywood, Charles Moyer, and George Pettibone, were accused of ordering the murder of Frank Steunenberg, former governor of Idaho. They were "kidnapped" by the state from Colorado without legal extradition procedures. Harry Orchard, a shadowy figure, admitted he had placed the bomb that killed Steunenberg but testified that the three labor leaders directed the murder. Many sympathetic to the miners believed that his confession was coerced.

Clarence Darrow was the defense attorney for Haywood, Moyer, and Pettibone, and the trial got wide coverage, notably in the *International Socialist Review*. Haywood and Moyer were acquitted, and charges against Pettibone were eventually dropped. Orchard was convicted to life in prison. The Socialists believed the trial was orchestrated to portray the Wobbly leaders as dangerous anarchists in order to discredit the WFM, the IWW, and the radical labor movement.

Quickly, Matilda and David grasped the nuances of Socialist theory, aligning themselves with the younger, radical members. She was one of only a few independent, single women, and she accepted a leadership role.

Between 1911 and 1915 there were over one hundred cities in the United States that elected Socialist mayors. Matilda applies the derisive term "municipal sewage plant" or "post-office" Socialist to the Socialist mayor Jasper McLevy, elected in Bridgeport years after she had moved to Los Angeles. The term was applied to Socialists concerned with reform, rather than those that advocated radical change. Socialist mayor George Lunn of Schenectady went to Little Falls to support the strikers Matilda organized in 1912. Clippings from the local papers show him being arrested in Little Falls along with three other supporters of the strike.

6 I FELL IN LOVE WITH HIM

The group that plugged for industrial unionism, that promoted the *International Socialist Review*, and that spent its pennies to turn out the *Industrial Unionist* was a young group, that is, young men; I was the only young woman in the group. There were some women members in the SP local, but they were older and married and shared the opinions of their husbands. While our local was divided on the question of industrial unionism and at issue on party questions, we were friendly in general activities—as Socialists. We worked together for successful May Days with their picnics and meetings and speakers; there was a Socialist Sunday Forum and socials where revolutionary poetry was read and little plays performed. And Ben Légère, a handsome young activist and a dynamic speaker, formed the Drama Club. I fell in love with him. The year was 1911, and we were both 24.

Ben was born in Massachusetts and grew up in Bridgeport. Both parents were Catholics—his mother Irish, an immigrant from County Cork, and his father French-Canadian. He had been sent to a parochial school and then for two years to high school. His father died when he was 14, and his mother ran a rooming house to support herself and the younger children. His older brother joined the navy at 17 and remained in the service until he died at about 50. I never met him, or Ben's three sisters. His mother I met only once or twice.

He married at 18. At the time we met he had two children. He held some poorly paid job as a cost clerk in a local factory, which hardly gave them even a poor living. His wife's family was helping some. Periodically, when things got too bad, they would move in with the in-laws. Young, intelligent, and healthy, Ben was nevertheless without work all too frequently. He hated factory work, but he had no special skill and so he drifted from job to job. What he was looking for was work in the theater; a playwright, a stage manager, and an actor, he lived in green-room illusions. At the time this fecklessness meant little to me; I was far more impressed with his outstanding activity in the SP, his ability to speak and hold his place in a debate with our opponents. We were partisans together.

I had become very active myself in the SP and was elected Women's State Correspondent, an office that emphasized work among the women's auxiliaries: promoting programs, coordinating activities, and so forth. Thus, I was a delegate to the 1911 SP convention held in New Haven. The convention was a stormy one, the hot question on the agenda being industrial unionism. The contest between its advocates and obstructionists provided a dramatic challenge to the sedate progress of the party. The entire industrial unionism block was charged with creating dissension, and about 40 members from a number of locals in Connecticut were expelled. Because I was an elected officer I could not be expelled without some special action by the membership. But I resigned.

I was loath to return to Bridgeport. My association with Ben naturally gave rise to gossip. My parents were grossly unhappy over the turn my life had taken: the absorption with Socialism, and now this affair with a married man.... I wanted to get away from it all—all, including Ben. So, when the convention was over I got on a train for Boston. Ben went back to Bridgeport.

I knew no one in Boston, had never been there. But I carried a WTUL membership card, and I went to its address directly from the station. The League occupied a small brick house on Warrenton Street, one of the oldest sections of Boston. I found the secretary, Mabel Gillespie, still in the office (her living quarters must have been in

the building), and I inquired about a room. I had very little money and hoped for as cheap a place as possible. "Could you do with a little attic room in the house?" she asked. "It will be only a dollar and a half a week, and there is the use of the kitchen." What luck! So I became a resident in the WTUL house for the next six months.

I arrived on a Friday. On Monday morning, having marked several garment shops advertising for help, I set out in search of a job. A small shop in East Boston, specializing in custom-made shirtwaists, tried

out my skill and hired me at $12 a week. The hours were from seven to six, but there was no Saturday work because of the Sabbath observance of the owner.

Ben had come up to Boston several weeks after I got there. He had had no job in Bridgeport for some time. He averred that something was going to turn up in the theater, something he was going to do with the play he had written, something he was going to publish, something was going to be performed. All fell through. Much later I learned that such things were always falling through. But that was much later.

Ben had barely enough money for the train fare from Bridgeport. He swore he'd try to get work, any kind of work, immediately. In the meantime I paid his room rent. He did get a clerical job in some factory at a pittance of a wage, not enough for a decent room and adequate food. The weekends were usually at my expense. I would pack a lunch early on Sunday, and we would set out by street car for the Blue Hills, about ten miles from Boston, or for some other spot away from the city. We were both fond of walking and often would walk many miles through the countryside. Once we made the trip on foot from the outskirts of Boston to Concord, a distance of some 25 miles. Once we walked from Brockton to Taunton, where Ben was born, a distance of 18 miles. So we spent our free time together. We were in love.

We spent some Sundays at the Socialist local, where there were often lectures, meetings of one sort or another, and where debates and discussions occurred on the issues that were agitating the Socialist Party at the time. It was the time of Socialist Clubs in the universities and colleges. Nearby Harvard had one, and so did Radcliffe. Some of the young students from both schools would be seen and heard at the meetings. They were imbued with the Socialist ideal; they had enormous respect for "working" Socialists. They were, in later years, to be found among the most radical of the American intelligentsia. These months were engaging months for me, socially, intellectually, and in my work.

On the personal level, they were disturbing months. Ben and I could neither live together nor live apart. He had never established a proper home for his family, and he was obviously running away from his responsibilities. I made no demands upon him, but neither did I step out of the situation, nor did I insist on a solution. I drifted along with the drifter. Better not to think. I, too, was running away.

It was pleasant living at the WTUL home. I could get my own meals, usually the evening meal, breakfast being a pickup on the way to work. There was a library and, two or three evenings a week, trade union activities. It was there I met for the first time Sara Conboy, business agent for the United Textile Workers (AFL), who was to become my adversary some years later in the South where I was organizing textile workers. A few weeks later Marie Hourwich, who was to become my closest friend, took up her residence at the League home. There were three or four rooms on the second floor made available to young women who had some professional connection with the League; mine was the only attic room.

Marie had come to work as a statistician on the newly formed Massachusetts Minimum Wage Commission. A survey of conditions among women workers in candy factories, department stores, and laundries was being made, preparatory to introducing a minimum wage law. Mabel Gillespie was one of the commissioners, Sara Conboy was another, and as near as I can remember, Mrs. Elizabeth G. Evans, years later to become known for her work on the Nicola Sacco and Bartolomeo Vanzetti case, was the chair.

Marie had graduated from Johns Hopkins University with a degree in economics, and this was her first job. She was the daughter of Dr. Isaac Hourwich, a well-known economist and author of an important book on immigration and labor. Marie had been born in Russia and graduated from gymnasium there before coming to the U.S. She had difficulty overcoming an accent, which made her self-conscious. Admiring my English, she sought my help. From the very beginning, we spent time together, reading, talking, taking walks in the public gardens, and sometimes going to lectures in Ford Hall. Within two months I became her assistant.

It came about fortuitously. My job in the shirtwaist shop came to an end after two months, slack season having set in. Nothing was

immediately available, and I began to worry. Finally, I told Miss Gillespie that I was unemployed. She questioned me as to my schooling and seemed surprised that it had ended with eighth grade.

"I was under the impression that you had much more education than that," she told me. "Have you ever done any clerical work? No, only factory work? Well, no matter. I think you may be able to help Miss Hourwich with her statistical work—and Miss Hourwich will doubtless want to help you." She knew we were friends. So it was that I was put on the staff at $50 a month.

Marie was a good teacher, and I was a diligent pupil. I was also something of a curiosity to the young college graduates—Wellesley, Radcliffe, Smith—who came to do the survey. An untutored immigrant girl, not a dozen years in the land, commanding an acquired language, grasping economics and the industrial conditions they were trying to survey. Yes, I was a curiosity, a creature of another world. Among them was one, Charlotte Claflin, a Bryn Mawr graduate, who seemed from the beginning to understand the conditions that sent such as me to work at 14 or younger, so that others, such as she, could have comforts and advantages, education and travel. She was a sensitive, gentle girl, keenly interested in the world beyond her own well-to-do social class.

On December 1, 1911, James and John McNamara confessed to the dynamiting of the *Los Angeles Times* printing plant. The labor movement, Socialists, and supporters of their defense were stunned by the confession. Even Samuel Gompers had been convinced that the brothers had been framed. I stood rooted, unbelieving, in front of the *Boston Herald* bulletin board amid a small crowd equally shocked, reading the news. Charlotte chanced to go by, stopped to read the news, and spotted me, as well. I must have shown my state of emotional shock. She pulled me away gently from the spot and walked me to the public gardens, where we continued walking for some time and then sat talking in the warmth of a lovely late autumn afternoon. Charlotte was a Unitarian. A year later during the long grim strike at

Little Falls she sent a brief note and a small gift, an aluminum folding cup, "in the name of the carpenter's son." She remains a bright thread in the fabric of my memory of those early years in Boston.

I doubt that I would have been noticed by these college-bred daughters of the New England gentry had it not been that I knew some of the languages spoken by the women being interviewed in the laundries and candy factories. The department store workers all spoke English, of course. But among the others were immigrants: Russians, Poles, Slovenes, and Finns, where language was a barrier to the interview. Although Marie Hourwich and I both spoke Russian, she could not often be spared to go out in the field with the investigators. In addition to Russian, I could manage well enough in Polish, Slovak, and Ukrainian, so I was asked to go along as interpreter where needed. The thing that intrigued the field workers, however, was my command of English, even a New England–accented English. How did I come by it? I could not quite tell them. Reading, listening, stock company theater, an elderly scholar who came to Socialist meetings and spoke exquisitely beautiful English, all of these probably contributed. I couldn't say how my ear absorbed the language, and after all I had been in the country more than a decade. But still—an eighth-grade education, a factory worker—I was a curiosity.

At the end of December the field survey was finished. The statistics were compiled, and the findings were submitted for evaluation to the commission's experts. Marie was offered another job with the Connecticut Industrial Commission, which was beginning a study of women in that state, and I returned to Bridgeport. Of course leaving Ben in Boston and returning to Bridgeport solved nothing. Sooner or later he would also return.

Our reunion was to be delayed by more cataclysmic events. Early in January the Lawrence strike broke out. Twenty-five thousand mill workers walked off the job in a spontaneous revolt against the intolerable conditions in the mills. I had left Boston only a few days before, and almost at once Ben was in Lawrence. Here was an opportunity for him at last to become a labor leader. That was what Ben wanted to be, at any rate, one of the things he wanted to be. He also wanted to be an actor, a playwright, an editor, a famous somebody. I was never able to learn just what it was that happened in Lawrence in 1912—why the leadership Ben sought eluded him. The strike lasted nine weeks. The leaders Joe Ettor and Arturo Giovannitti were arrested early on and jailed for months awaiting trial. Other leaders came and went and became notorious, but Ben went unnoticed. It was not until almost the end of that year and in another strike that he achieved his goal, and his name as strike leader made the headlines in the Bridgeport newspapers.

I had intended to return to the factory after my brief experience in white-collar work in Boston. That was an avenue of employment which I had neither the skill nor the desire to continue. But shortly after my return Marie Hourwich wrote to say that she had recommended me for a position as her assistant in the statistical work she was doing, and that I could have the job at $75 a month. Certainly it was better wages and conditions than the corset factory, and I was thirsty for new experiences and anxious to leave Bridgeport. A conflict was imminent in the "triangle" which my affair with Ben had formed, so I left for Hartford.

The Connecticut Industrial Commission survey had employed some of the same workers I had known in Boston, and a number of new ones. I served in much the same capacity as I had on the Minimum Wage Survey. In this new survey the women and miners in the metal industries were being studied. And here too, my languages were useful. Marie and I had rooms at the YWCA. The staff worked in the capitol building. The survey took about four months.

During my stay in Hartford the case of Ettor and Giovannitti emerged as the most important labor defense case. These IWW organizers were charged with inciting to riot in a picket line when the striker Anna LoPizzo was killed by the police. Scores of labor organizers and speakers were traveling the country on behalf of the two

Lawrence strike leaders, who were in jail. Ben was active in the defense
work, and I gave what time I could spare from my job. On occasional
weekends we encountered one another on a speaking assignment or at
a meeting in some New England town, and naturally we were drawn
together personally.

As the Connecticut Industrial Commission survey was terminat-
ing, a study of infant mortality was being initiated by the Federal Children's Bureau in Waterbury, Connecticut. I was asked to remain on the
staff at the same pay with the same duties—statistical assistant and
interpreter. Again Marie and I found rooms together in Waterbury
where the fieldwork was going on. The work was completed in early
October, and some of the staff, including Marie, went on to Washington for compilation and evaluation. I went back to Bridgeport.

This time I brought back a new idea of what I wanted to do. I wanted to go to college. The idea was born of a friendship with one of the
field-workers in the infant mortality study, Marie Kasten. Her home
was in Madison, Wisconsin, and she was a graduate of the University

of Wisconsin there. She was a frail, reserved young woman, apparently in poor health. Beyond the work on the study, she seemed to have little energy. She rarely went out socially, pleading fatigue, and she always retired early. But she liked to talk to me and of an evening would invite me to her room. Almost always lying down and with the light turned low, she never spoke of herself, but liked to hear of my experiences as an immigrant and a factory worker. Like some of the others, she was intrigued by my command of English, the amount of reading I had done, and my radicalism. She felt that I should aim at something higher than factory work and convinced me that with some preparation I could be accepted as a special student at the University of Wisconsin. If I could get some instruction in mathematics and perhaps some Latin, she said, with what I had already acquired in history and literature, she was sure I would have a very good chance. She thought that I could work my way by getting a job in the library, where she seemed to be well connected. The idea was new, and I was skeptical at first, but with her urging and offers of assistance when I got to Madison, I came to accept it.

I had saved a few dollars, perhaps 50 or 60, and decided to put that into the necessary studies by immediately engaging a student in Bridgeport to tutor me. His fee was two dollars a lesson! At two lessons a week my savings would cover only a brief period, but once again I could get a job in a corset factory. Indeed, I would try to get a job at once to take care of my share of the family living expenses. Such was my plan. I was quite excited over this new turn in my life. But it came to a short stop.

BEN LÉGÈRE MUST HAVE SEEN THE ARTICLES MATILDA wrote for the *Bridgeport Herald*, and since she was an elected officer in the Bridgeport Socialist Party, he must have known who she was.

She doesn't appear to have saved tear sheets or clippings of her published articles or stories. In fact, others saved the clippings I have. Ben, in contrast, hoarded his clippings and strangely gave some of them to me, so I have a few articles and other documents that help me to see and feel their time, and learn something more than Matilda reveals.

Though she says she never met Ben's sisters, their names, "Miss Mae Legere" and "Miss Florence Legere," are listed among the actors on one of the programs from *The Educational Stage* at Warner Hall, Bridgeport, in 1911; she must have seen them perform. Ben gave these playbills to me a half century ago. One of the programs lists both Matilda and David Rabinowitz as actors in another of Ben's productions, Ibsen's *Master Builder*, by the Bridgeport Progressive Dramatic Association, in the summer of 1911 (Ben was the male lead, Matilda the female). She doesn't refer to her brief stint as an actor. Perhaps this is another example of her natural reticence or her disdain for the cult of personality that so influenced Ben.

When I visited the Labor Archives in the Walter Reuther Library at Wayne State University in Detroit and looked through Matilda Robbins's small collection and Ben's more voluminous one, I found Ben's archive packed with personal correspondence and ephemera. He typed many of his letters to his children, sisters, and wives. It amused me to find not only their letters to him, but many of his letters to them, as he kept carbon copies of much of his correspondence—great for the researcher, and an indication of the self-consciousness of the writer.

Ben had two daughters at the time he and Matilda met, Elaine and his firstborn, Benita, named after himself. Many years later Ben's fourth wife gave birth to his only son, Benny (also named after his father). During the course of Matilda's relationship with him, Ben's legal wife, who, like one of his sisters, was also named Florence and sometimes called "Flo" or "Flora," produced their third daughter, Jane. So while my grandparents were involved with each other, Ben still spent at least some nights in the matrimonial bed. As one would expect for an advocate of the "free love idea," Matilda doesn't admit to objecting to the arrangement. As she assured me in the 1960s when we briefly discussed their relationship, "Of course I was free to do the same."

In fact, much about Ben's character appears to elude her through the years of their tumultuous affair. It is hard to understand how she could have been so critical of the foibles of some of the Socialists and Wobblies among her acquaintances and yet have overlooked for so long Ben's many shortcomings. She paid his room rent while he looked for work. Time spent together on Matilda's days off was, she writes, "at my expense." Here and throughout, she contrasts, with some pride, Ben's perpetual penury and her ability to manage. She lent him money, gave him shelter, and paid for restaurant meals, train trips, and streetcar fares. She provided not only for him, but also for his daughters when he brought them to her for visits. In retrospect, she saw what a freeloader and a cad he was, but she was silent about her reasons for continuing the decade-long relationship.

What courage it must have taken to strike out for Boston, knowing no one there, and how brave she was to present herself at the WTUL office with only her membership card for entrée. She was amazingly plucky throughout her life. She wasn't shy to ask for work or lodging for herself and her child, or support for the strikers she organized and the political prisoners that she championed. Although she was assertive, she assiduously avoided making herself the subject of any issue she championed. Perhaps that is why she saved so little of her written work and why historians overlooked her contributions for decades. She did not publish a memoir as did Elizabeth Gurley Flynn, Emma Goldman, or Big Bill Haywood. She didn't go to the highly visible, "important" strikes, but slogged it out in Little Falls, Shelton, Detroit, and South Carolina. It was never about her; it was about the workers, the cause, and much of the work depleted and exhausted her.

Her job in the shirtwaist factory was eleven hours a day, so she had two days off, "because of the Sabbath observance of the owner." Still, she worked a fifty-five-hour week and, of course, got no overtime pay for long, tedious, deadening, extra hours of work each day. Then, as usual, she was laid off during the slack season. This turned out to be fortunate, since it occasioned her entry into much more interesting and fulfilling work that made excellent use of her intelligence, diligence, and curiosity. Marie Hourwich (later Kravitz) became a lifelong friend and introduced her to a world of educated, principled women with jobs in government, whose surveys led to the adoption of regulatory measures that alleviated some of the more extreme abuses of the economic system.

Matilda's fearlessness and intellectual abilities were astonishing. She describes the usefulness of her facility with Russian, Polish, Ukrainian, and Slovak languages on the Massachusetts Minimum Wage Commission survey, but she makes no mention of her need to use Yiddish. Surely there were situations where she must have been called upon to use her mother tongue.

The McNamara brothers' confession to bombing the *Los Angeles Times* building at year's end was a terrible blow to Matilda and her fellow radicals who believed the McNamaras had been framed. A month later, the Lawrence strike began, and she returned to Bridgeport, but only briefly.

While Ben hastened to Lawrence, she resumed work with Marie Hourwich, this time for the Connecticut Industrial Commission survey. She is not explicit about the "conflict" and the "triangle" caused by the affair with Ben, and this reticence in personal matters is characteristic. She tells us nearly nothing. We must imagine the trysts— her living at home with her disapproving parents, and he living with his wife and children, or perhaps with his family and his in-laws. Where did they meet to carry on their romance? How did she deal with the discomfort she felt in her personal life?

She says she returned to Bridgeport in October with the idea of going to college and describes engaging a tutor to fill the gaps in her limited education, ending as it did in the eighth grade. Perhaps she developed this plan to flee from the "triangle," and maybe she was driven more by the desire to escape than the desire for a college education. It appears that only a month elapsed before the plan was abandoned and she moved on to assume the great challenges she would undertake in the next decade.

7   LITTLE FALLS

The Lawrence strike produced a great impetus to the organization of textile workers throughout the Northeast and elsewhere. Among the numerous mill towns where strikes were breaking out was Little Falls, New York. In early November 1912, 1,600 mill workers struck there. Organizers and speakers were greatly needed, and Ben and an Italian-speaking organizer, Filippo Bocchini, were sent there. Ten days after they arrived a typical flare-up took place on a picket line, and 14, including Ben and Bocchini, were arrested and jailed. The Bridgeport papers carried a prominent notice of Ben's arrest. We were then both members of the IWW, which was in charge of the strike. I wired the IWW office in Chicago for confirmation, and that same day came a telegram from the secretary, Vincent Saint John: "Go to Little Falls at once. Name N. O. as authority."

A new and unpredictable road lay ahead. Early the next day I called my tutor, packed my grip, and, to the dismay of my parents, left for Little Falls. I had never been in a strike. My short and unsuccessful effort to interest corset workers in a union was hardly even a beginning in the art of labor organization. To be sure, I knew both firsthand

113

and in the contacts with scores of women workers interviewed in the surveys in Massachusetts and Connecticut what the conditions were and how justified any strike would be. I had also read Socialist and labor literature and formed ideas. But to be cast suddenly into a role of responsibility for a strike was rather frightening.

Traveling all day, I took a train from Bridgeport to New York City, then changed to the N.Y. Central Railroad bound for Albany. From there I took a branch line to Little Falls. I was both stimulated and oppressed. It was a long and tedious ride, and it was dark as the three-car train finally puffed into the dimly lit station at Little Falls. As the train was slowly pulling in and the few passengers to embark were gathering their things, I became aware of two busy-looking men going through the car I was in and peering about and into the faces of the passengers. They hopped off as the train stopped and stood hard by the steps sharply watching the descending passengers. Having read and heard descriptions of "reception committees," where labor organizers were met at trains and prevented from stopping, I guessed who these men were looking for. They had hardly a glance for me. Since it was Thanksgiving Eve, I imagine they dismissed me as a youngster coming home for the holiday.

Fearing to draw attention to myself, I walked off the platform without asking for directions to the headquarters of the strike, Sokol Hall. I followed some people along the more lighted streets, hoping they would lead to a street car, but there were no street cars in Little Falls in 1912. Once or twice I heard Slovenian spoken. I knew the town was on the Mohawk River, and the speakers were headed toward a row of lights that suggested a bridge. I let one or two pass, then hearing another speak Slovenian, I asked him for directions to Sokol Hall. He said he was going to a meeting there, so I introduced myself. My escort brought me into a crowded hall where apparently I had been expected, but since the Chicago IWW office's wire had not specified the time of my arrival, they had not sent anyone to meet me.

It was about nine o'clock. The meeting had been going on for two

or three hours. The strikers—Czechs, Poles, and Italians—were listening to a report on the day's strike activities. There was a little flurry of excitement as the young striker motioned to the speaker. He interrupted his report, introduced me, and the warm greeting of the strikers brought tears to my eyes. I wanted to say something light, something cheery. To hide my discomfort, I told them of the two dicks and how they ignored me. That made them laugh and helped me to regain my composure. So my tough, 14-week task in Little Falls began.

I sat with the strike committee after the general meeting adjourned and was informed of events from the beginning. Conditions were as bad as they had been in Lawrence: a 55-hour week, miserable pay, the speed-up, abuses of various kinds—a spontaneous walk-out as in Lawrence. The procedure in IWW strikes in those days was pretty much the same; organization was new, and there was never a treasury.

A number of bright young men and women on the strike committee had managed to hold the strike together. Picketing had continued even after the attack by the police and the arrest of the leaders, but

after two weeks the strikers had exhausted what tiny reserves they had. They were helping each other as best they could, but a common commissary and kitchen was urgently needed. We had to find money for it and volunteers to manage it. Legal aid was also needed for those in jail, and we had to immediately organize publicity and send out appeals for help.

Offered an attic room in the house of a striker, I rose early shivering in the unheated room, washed, if the water had not frozen, and along with the strikers made the picket line at 6 a.m. I found the daily picket line in the bitter cold a test of endurance and marveled at the courage of the poorly clad strikers, who kept their spirits up with humor and song in the Wobbly tradition.

Stamping through snow, our breath steam, we circled the mills and circled the mills and often sang. Italian blended well with the Polish and Slavic revolutionary labor songs—there was hope and courage in them.

Soon IWW attorney Fred Moore arrived to handle the legal issues. Twelve of the 14 arrested were released after a few days in jail, but Ben and Bocchini were charged with inciting to riot and held without bail. Phillips Russell, a well-known labor journalist, arrived to do turn-out publicity. To feed the strikers we dispatched appeals for funds to unions, Socialist Party locals, and sympathetic individuals. The commissary was set up for distribution of groceries to families, while single persons were fed in its hall.

Although it was the women strikers alone who toiled long hours in the kitchen, both men and women worked in the adjoining shop to clean and repair the arriving donations of clothing. Two Italian cobblers did wonders with worn shoes. It was a busy little world, struggling to survive. And yet what an example it was that men and women of different backgrounds, and speaking different languages, could strive together against great odds in unbroken solidarity for three months, determined to wrest a little more life for themselves and their children.

For me the days and the nights were crowded with work. The picket

line at six in the morning. Coffee, bread, and perhaps some stewed fruit after that at the commissary. The daily meeting with the strike committee in the forenoon with a report on the response to appeals, funds, developments. Correspondence and bookkeeping; details of the office.

A general meeting was held for all strikers every night at Sokol Hall, and once a week a social get-together with a fiddle or a harmonium for dancing and singing.

The winter was severe. The Mohawk Valley was beautiful, white and sparkling with snow. Long icicles hung from trees, and the sound of sleigh bells tinkled merrily in the crisp air, but oh, how cold it was!

And what of Ben, languishing in jail as the weeks dragged into months? Twice a week I made the trip to Herkimer, about eight miles away, to visit the two prisoners in the county jail there. There was a limit on the time I could stay, and of course I spent most of the time with Ben. Both he and Bocchini were very agitated during my visits, and of course they were miserably unhappy. Their arrest had come too quickly, too suddenly, they complained. They had hardly gotten into the strike. It had been their first one, too. They had hardly gotten to know the strikers, to merit their confidence, to develop organization when they were picked off. Bocchini, emotional, had little theory or practice in organization and was filled with romantic ideas about anarchism, but he was nevertheless more amiable, more appreciative of the tasks the strike demanded of me, more considerate of my load.

Ben, in addition to the chagrin at his short-lived leadership and at the loss of his freedom, believed he had a personal claim on me. He was truculent, officious, and wildly jealous of me. He insisted that I heed and act upon his ideas about the strike, dismissing any of my ideas or those of other members of the strike committee, and he was suspicious of every man to whom I made even a passing reference. I dreaded those visits more and more. Those days, so utterly lost, left me feeling spent and almost ill.

Then suddenly Big Bill Haywood was among us. His arrival caused quite a sensation among the strikers, but I remember him sitting in an

old office chair rather too small for his big, slack body, his arms hanging limp over the arms of the chair, his good eye a bit cocked, smoking one cigarette after another. To me he seemed to lack repose, concentration, patience. Criticism upset him, and he defended even his small mistakes heatedly. He could not write. But I remember his veiled chagrin when his composition of a leaflet or a pamphlet was corrected by a well-educated fellow worker who had been doing our publicity. He felt himself a keen observer of men's motives and claimed to be able to spot an informer anywhere. But at least in Little Falls he was taken in by one who brought us much trouble during the subsequent trial of one of the organizers. The informer professed to be a friend of the strikers and was jailed briefly and released. He came to see Bill, bringing him a letter from the organizer, thus gaining his confidence. After that letters went back and forth between the organizer and his sweetheart. The organizer had a wife and a sweetheart. During the trial copies of these letters were introduced to show moral turpitude. They no doubt contributed to the prejudices of the judge and jury. Years later when I mentioned this to Bill, he made an impatient gesture and told me to forget it.

During his week with us in Little Falls he walked in the picket line two or three times, his figure looming large, his head with its large hat above the men and women who followed. (Since I am under five feet tall and he was over six feet, we were sometimes referred to as the long and the short of the strike.) Mill detectives kept an eye on him. The townspeople whispered as he passed. The local newspaper fulminated daily against this terrible agitator. His reputation preceded him. And I learned early how reputations can be made by both friends and foes. And once a reputation is made legends grow up around it. Writers, especially, practice the gift of building legends.

But the men and women, activists and sympathizers from near and far, who came to Little Falls, served, and remained unknown, were to me the true heroes of that far-off day. Here a minister who left church-ianity for Christianity and managed our commissary; a writer who volunteered to do our publicity; a sociologist who drew our posters and took care of our printing; these and others mixed and worked and suffered with the mill workers. They came unbidden, and they left unknown. And across the years and with a rare nostalgia, I remember them.

After seeing these men and women at work, the Great Man was disappointing. I had not met him until that time, but to me as to most of our youth, he was the symbol of militant unionism, of organizing genius, of revolutionary ardor. His arrival in Little Falls created a stir. Just as the dicks paid no attention to me when I arrived at the railroad station, so in contrast were they and the town policemen lined up on the platform and on the alert as he stepped off the train. And after that for the ten days that he stayed with us he was shadowed. He marched with us in the picket line, and the strikers admired him. He could not speak the language of the older ones, but he had fun dancing with the younger ones. He talked a great deal to us in committee meetings, but in the end I felt the lack of constructive value in what he said. Already I had learned much from the concise directives in Vincent Saint John's letters. The man's analytical ability, his orderly thinking and clear-cut phrasing, built for me the strongest foundation upon which much of my future work rested. The tutelage of Bill Haywood left me nothing to draw on. Of the thousands of words he uttered I recalled very few. There must have been times and situations that created Bill Haywood's famed personality and revealed his unique talents. I did not find them. I could not draw strength from his past exploits. It was the present that challenged. And in the present his approach lacked vigor and his methods realism.

What precisely was his contribution? Was it the ineffable aura of a much publicized personality? Yes, he was impressive physically. He was noticed wherever he went, but where was the substance? Was it the beginning of his decline? No. There was Paterson still to come. And the war. And the mass trial of the IWW in 1917.

It is not my intention here to deflate reputations. Certainly Bill made a large contribution to militant unionism. He became famous in 1907 when he, with Moyer and Pettibone, was tried and acquitted on the charge of murdering Governor Steunenberg of Idaho. He was with the IWW from its inception and general secretary for some years. He was a key figure in the Lawrence strike, and in the Paterson strike. He was a famed labor agitator. In the mass trial of the IWW in 1917 he was the center of attention and the leader among the 117 men brought to trial. That he was later to jump his $40,000 bail bond and flee to Russia, even the wildest imagination of his most implacable enemies would dare not conceive.

When he came to Little Falls he was at the height of his labor career. And yet, as I observed him during the days he spent close to me at strike headquarters, I felt the weakness of the man. He wrote a leaflet and talked at length about the current and past strikes and organizational drives; he made some short speeches in English, which had to be translated into Italian, Polish, and Czech, and then he was gone.

Perhaps I was too impressed with Haywood's famous trial, his militant speeches, his part in the Lawrence strike. His fame at this time was perhaps at its apogee. Being young in the organization and a bit romantic, I probably indulged in unrealistic ideas of what revolutionary labor leaders should be. Eugene Debs influenced me, and the simple stern devotion of Saint John, and especially those who had come to Little Falls to give of themselves, their small means, expecting no reward.

The strike dragged on through the many weeks. After the first arrests, there were continuous intimidations of the pickets. The police invaded Sokol Hall and made a shambles of it, but none broke ranks. And when the strike was settled in February, even though the gains were small, the 1,600 mill workers were proud in their solidarity.

The 14 weeks I spent in Little Falls were perhaps the most memorable of my entire career as a labor organizer. First, it was the most intense training period one could undergo, and I quickly learned about the many-faceted duties of a strike. It was my first big challenge. Then, because the strike was concentrated in a small town (Little Falls had probably no more than a population of 10,000 at that time) we who came to help lived close to the strikers, spoke and worked only with them and for them. Some were more involved, some less, but I soon learned to observe and to distinguish sincerity from show, capability from bluster.

From the beginning and throughout the strike my mentor was Vincent Saint John, the general secretary of the IWW. It was he who signed the telegram that sent me to Little Falls, and his letters, clear, concise, friendly, and austere, became and remained my model for intelligent correspondence—the basis for a concentrated course in labor organization. He was an efficient executive, a shrewd labor organizer, a sensitive social thinker—an intransigent revolutionist. I met him only once, in New York, on my way home from Little Falls. He was with a group of people discussing organization. He said less than any of them, but always his words, with their simplicity and clarity, held the attention and respect of the listeners.

Ben's trial was soon to begin, so when I left Little Falls in February the IWW headquarters approved a tour for me for the purpose of raising funds for the Légère-Bocchini defense. Ben and I parted abruptly, following the last of many tempestuous and agonizing visits in the Herkimer jail. I never saw Bocchini again. Although he was in a highly emotional state, our parting was comradely, and he was grateful for the little I had done for him. Ben played the martyr role, and I left him in a flood of bitter discontent and suspicion. While he played the role, as well, of great labor leader, my fellow workers, even on short acquaintance in Little Falls, seemed to have little respect for his ability or integrity. I went through much torment and disappointment, but my vision of him was not so clear then as it would later become,

and I still condoned much. I was determined to make the separation complete, however, and though I would do everything possible for the defense, I would sever all intimate contact. I was determined that our romance was finished. Was I still in love with him? It was a question I could not then answer.

WHERE ARE THE WOMEN?

The years 1911 to 1913 were anxious ones for Matilda—factory worker, nascent Socialist, and new member of the IWW. In March 1911 the Triangle Shirtwaist fire galvanized labor and deeply disturbed Matilda, as it did even those not particularly sympathetic to labor. It outraged workers in the textile and garment industry and anyone who sympathized with workers or held anticapitalist views. Then came the Lawrence, Massachusetts, strike in May 1912 where Matilda's comrade Joe Ettor and fellow Wobbly Arturo Giovannitti were arrested along with Joseph Caruso, who was not a Wobbly. They were framed for the murder of striker Anna LoPizzo, who was probably killed by the police during the violence that erupted during the Lawrence strike. Finally Ettor's and Giovannitti's prosecutions were separated from Caruso's, while Matilda and Ben became more and more involved with the defense, the IWW, and each other.

Fred Moore, the IWW's defense attorney, was a friend. I remember my grandmother describing, when I was in high school, Moore's defense of Sacco and Vanzetti in the early phase of their ordeal. I was writing a paper for my history class and had selected a famous trial of the early twentieth century. She described attending the trial as a secretary for the Socialist Party and meeting with the defendants. Vanzetti deeply impressed her, but she didn't find Sacco sympathetic and suspected he might have been guilty. Years later, searching the Internet for clues, I found an MP3 reading of Matilda's writing about visiting Vanzetti in jail. The piece is printed in Joyce Kornbluth's *Rebel Voices: An IWW Anthology.**

Reticent as always about the details of her personal life, Matilda doesn't comment on her relationship with Moore, but my mother believed that she and Fred Moore were lovers in the mid- to late 1920s. Moore may have been married at this time, but this would have made little difference to those that adhered to the free love ideal. Vita remembered traveling by car from St. Louis to Los Angeles with him at the wheel most of the time, although sometimes he disappeared for days or even weeks, taking his Stetson and Matilda's typewriter, returning with neither. Matilda did tell my mother that Moore was

*Joyce Kornbluth, *Rebel Voices: An IWW Anthology* (repr. Oakland, CA: PM Press, 2011), 360.

probably a cocaine user, and other sources confirm this. Whatever her relationship with Fred, Fred's brother, Channing Moore, and his wife, whom Vita called "Aunt Bea," remained friends and gave Matilda support over the years. Vita remembered with nostalgia the summers that her mother ran a camp for girls on the Moore's ranch in Escondido, California.

On the heels of the Lawrence strike, another mill town, Little Falls, was thrown into chaos by the state of New York's new labor laws that cut the workers' hours to fifty-four a week, instead of the usual sixty. Little Falls was a small city with over sixty manufacturing concerns, but the Gilbert and Phoenix knitting mills were the two largest employers in the town. Eventually over 1,200 went out on strike.

Today Little Falls, on the Mohawk River along the Erie Canal, like so many formerly industrial towns in the Northeast, struggles with the declining prosperity resulting from long-vanished industrial employment. When I visited one hundred years after Matilda's "most immemorial year," I learned how, in 1912, the mill bosses cut the workers' pay to equal the reduction in hours that the new laws decreed. The call went up, "Strike! Strike!" and the mill hands spontaneously walked out. Workers, most of them women and girls, struck both knitting mills in town. Scabs were hired at double the pay of the striking workers.

When IWW General Secretary Vincent Saint John authorized her to go to Little Falls after Ben and Bocchini were arrested, Matilda was just twenty-five years old, small, foreign-looking, untested in the art of labor organizing, Ben's comrade and lover, vibrating with ardor, ideals, and anxiety.

On the one-hundred-year anniversary, I joined a group of citizens in commemoration of the textile strike Matilda led. They knew about her. Members of the Little Falls Historical Society held a number of public events and displays about the strike. They arranged a tour of sites important during the strike, and costumed reenactors provided information and details throughout the city of Little Falls. One costumed woman told me she is the descendant of an Italian striker and that her daughter learned about the strike in the fourth grade. "And guess what she does now," she asked with pride; "She's a labor organizer!" Everyone warmly welcomed me, and they invited me to read from Matilda's memoir at a gathering in the art center. It is directly adjacent to one of the former mills, a handsome building now converted to commercial space, housing a restaurant, a bed and breakfast, an antiques mall, and a black box theater.

The next day I attended a play in the theater, a dramatization of the strike, where Matilda and Ben are major characters, along with someone I have never heard of—Miss Schloss. It surprised me to hear of another important woman leader, someone never mentioned in Matilda's account of the strike. Not a word about Helen Minnie Schloss, who urgently requested help from the IWW when the spontaneous strike occurred. As the strike progressed, Schloss helped manage the day-to-day operation. She went to jail in Little Falls, along with thirteen others, including Ben. Two women are depicted in a photo of the arrested strikers published in the *International Socialist Review*. I recognize Ben in front on the lower left, in his characteristic flowing tie, his arm casually draped around a women seated next to him and arrested with him. Could this have been Helen? She is said to be among those pictured.

A public health nurse, Helen Schloss was originally hired by the ladies of the Fortnightly Club, wives of the town's elite—mill bosses, business and political leaders, the police chief, and the fire chief. Schloss was engaged to minister to the workers in the tenements because of endemic tuberculosis, a disease that could have spread to the other side of the river if not controlled. When the strike occurred, Schloss summoned help and pitched in to organize picket lines and help out in the strikers' kitchen. She went on speaking tours in defense of Légère and Bocchini and spoke eloquently in support of the strikers to the press and to government agencies. She provided testimony to the Factory Investigating Committee of the New York

State Legislature about the unhealthy conditions for families in the tenements and invited them to Little Falls to see at first hand the deplorable conditions of the workers. She was, like Matilda, a Russian immigrant, although middle class with a college education, a graduate of the leftist Rand School of Social Science. She was sympathetic to the strikers and worked tirelessly in their interest.

Why does Matilda exclude her? Was she a romantic rival? A political foe? I wondered why a seeming ally would be written out of the account. Members of the historical society provided some clues. We were taken past the house where Schloss resided, a substantial structure owned by the family of one of the mill owners, on the "right side" of the tracks, across the canal and river from the part of town where the "foreign" workers lived. Here was evidence of another sort. Matilda describes many of those who came to support the strike and "lived close to the strikers." The contrast of that large, bourgeois house with the clapboard tenement where I later discovered my grandmother had rented a room made obvious the class difference between her and Schloss, and between Schloss and the workers.

Bob Albrecht, a member of the Little Falls Historical Society, who has researched Schloss's life, provided an additional suggestion for the omission. He told me that Schloss herself had written of her social isolation in Little Falls and of her chagrin at the workers' mistrust of her. She was a leftist and may have gone to Russia as a nurse after the revolution.

Matilda writes that there were always spies among the workers during strikes, and perhaps this outsider was suspect because she was not a member of the IWW and not known to anyone in Little Falls prior to her arrival. And although it is tempting to consider the possibility—knowing my grandfather's reputation—I don't think she was a romantic rival. Albrecht discovered that she had died, in 1965, in a New Jersey apartment she had shared for many years with another woman. I believe she was not interested in romantic attachments to men.

George Lunn, the Socialist mayor of Schenectady and a supporter of the strike, came to Little Falls with his wife and was arrested, too. Helen Keller sent a letter supporting the strike with a check, unmentioned in Matilda's account. Matilda sent appeals to sympathizers across the country and organized a mass departure of strikers' children for their health and protection to Socialist families outside of Little Falls. This tactic, developed during the Lawrence strike, proved again successful in gaining wide support for the strikers and, no doubt, the Légère-Bocchini Defense Committee. The police chief, Dusty Long, tried to prevent the children's exodus, but eventually they were allowed to leave.

In addition to attending to the strike, Matilda visited Ben in jail, taking the trolley to Herkimer, about ten miles away. On my visit, I was shown the jail and, from the outside, Ben and Bocchini's cell—second floor, last window. Matilda also spent time working on raising money and support for their defense. Her description of the daily work—the cold, the fatigue, the details of organizing support for the strike outside of Little Falls, feeding and clothing the workers—is counterpoint to her sketches of the Wobbly stars.

Big Bill Haywood and Carlo Tresca (who makes a brief appearance with his lover Elizabeth Gurley Flynn in a later chapter) disappoint with the slenderness of their contribution—speeches, picketing with the strikers, then festive restaurant dinners and the Saturday night social events where Haywood dances with the pretty girls and Tresca flirts in Italian. The violence of the police and the private detectives hired to break the strike was terrifying at times, and the presence of spies became evident. Police anticipated the strikers' tactics and imposed harsh measures to thwart them. Bigotry was rampant. "American" workers in the nearby bicycle and furniture factories shouted obscenities at the "foreign" strikers and hurled hammers and other missiles at picketers. Matilda rarely mentions violence, although she certainly encountered it. Women were the vanguard and the soul of this strike, and Matilda encouraged their participation in decision making and helped them organize the work, not only the picketing, but necessary support such as food preparation and clothing distribution. I can imagine her patiently explaining the legal issues and tactics, discussing Socialism and democracy with them, using her command of Yiddish or Slavic languages when necessary, nobly ignoring the crude taunts flung at her on the street.

Especially humiliating was the publication in the local papers of Ben and Matilda's love letters. In her memoir, she blames Haywood for being taken in by an informer. Who was the spy who betrayed them? Matilda's account describes the letters that passed between them, that were intercepted, then published in the local paper, as if the incident happened to someone else. She describes Ben as "one of the organizers" and says he "had a wife and a sweetheart." Matilda knew the wife. Matilda was the "sweetheart."

When I was a student at Berkeley, Ben sometimes invited me to see a play or took me to lunch or dinner. Once he invited me to join a play reading of *Major Barbara* with a group he belonged to. Another time he took me to lunch at Moar's Cafeteria in San Francisco, where art by his "friend Bennie Bufano" was exhibited.

On one of these "dates" he gave me playbills from the Bridgeport performances and old newspaper clippings of those love letters. I never mentioned this to my grandmother. Much later, after both of them were dead, I realized what unusual documents these clippings were. I still have those brittle shreds. Looking at them again, after my visit to Little Falls, I notice the address on Matilda's letter to Ben and realize that I had photographed that tenement house one hundred years after she had occupied the room in the attic. I realized precisely and with certainty where she "lived close to the strikers."

There are no dates on his clippings, but they were printed during Ben's trial in May 1913. These are the letters, the first from Ben to Matilda and the second from Matilda to Ben:

THE LITTLE FALLS EVENING TIMES

LOVE LETTERS FIGURE IN CASE

Wonderful Missives Found that May Be Used in Trial of Prisoners That Was Begun at Herkimer Today

A number of love letters have been found that will be used in the trial of some of the men now in Herkimer Jail who were arrested in connection with the local strike. The Times some time ago published a letter that occasioned much comment. The epistle given below is a masterful composition in English, a remarkable declaration of love, of self-abasement. It ranks even ahead of the Grace Brown letters that created such a sensation a few years ago and has very few equals even in the annals of literature. The letter is given herewith, as follows:

Herkimer County Jail.
Herkimer, N.Y. Nov. 29 1912

Dear Love: Today I feel immeasurably better than I have for days and days. Hope seems to begin once more to burn within me. For the first time since I have been here the pain has gone from my heart. I've been trying to understand it all morning. It seems so impossible that such a feeling should be. Especially when I think back over the night that has just past. How I suffered last night. When you were gone and again I was all alone my tired aching heart just broke within me. But something new seems to have been born of it. Some big sustaining thing. Let me first tell you what happened. It cannot hurt now because it is all over and will never come again. Never as long as I live. I've had my trial by fire and emerged this morning. Emerged, not triumphant, not inflated, nor scarless, not without the marks of the agony, not cheering myself on any longer: but clear-visioned. Unblinded. Nothing in me any longer shuts out the glory of you. Nothing in me ever can again. No, I have never said this before. It is not a renewal of any old vows. It is not a pledge I'm making. It is not [meant] to please you. It is not being said to bring joy to your dear [self?]. It is my revelation. I am telling you simply, very simply, what I have learned.

I am letting you know the sum of my suffering. I am just kneeling down and holding up my clasped hands, as I always did when I discovered you on [missing word] height. But this time there are [no words?] left. I do not kiss the hem of your gown this time. I do not kiss [word missing] of your foot nor the tips of your fingers. I just sink to my knees [missing word] world beneath you. I hold up [missing words] hands to let you gently [missing words] fingers round them, then [missing words] until the full fine light of [lots of missing words] ... drops of pure joy and exhaltation [sic] trembles on the lids, then rolls off to fall a showering baptism upon my upturned face. I can look up now and ask nothing, nothing at all because I know that always, always trembling slender fingers are stealing thro [sic] my hair, soft hands

bearing the full touch of the world's love stroke gently my flaming cheek and always, always, sweet warm lips seek mine in deepest passionate love. When the soft hands again plead gently with my tired frame to rise—to rise from my knees, I know that some hurts are healed forever and a new light shines in our lives—to light us on our path—together. The cell has fallen apart and I am alone in the world with you. Only the world enshrouds us and you there and I here together, Dear little girl, Matilda! Great soul!!

When you went last night all those things you said racked me. I walked and walked and suffered. Oh, I could have flung myself against the bars in fury and despair; but for my thumping brain which kept urging my staggering feet backward and forward, backward and forward on the endless floor of the cell from the window to the door. I walked steadily until 7:30 then flung myself into bed to writhe and twist and groan and try to shut out horrible visions. At last I slept for an hour or so.

Then at 10 I awoke in a horrible nightmare. So I rose and paced the floor in the dark until my body was tired again. Then I lay in bed. Always kept running thro [sic] my mind the worn figure sitting on the edge of my bed holding aloof from me tho [sic] consciousness of its own superior strength and my weakness. My cruel, blind, and selfish weakness. Then would always come three things which tortured me all night. Three visions flashing across my mind. 'Clark' a single word, a name, a monstrous thing, a great hideous calamity. I saw that terrible soul shrinking that was visible in you as you let me know that story. Then how I suffered. I here in chains. You there—and that.

Then came chasing on the heels of that one, a coarse, profane word falling from lips I love. Hell!!! Like a slip, like a break, a reversion so ominously familiar, so crushingly real, not put out for effect; but escaping from inward struggle—like an ugly wasp bursting from the agitated heart of a rose. It cut my soul. Sunk in and burned, leaving a white scar. That would not be you. In my troubled sleep I learned it was not you. Then came the chastening truth. 'See what you have done to her!' Over and over in my hours of agony came the thundering accusation from my soul. [missing words] [Over and over my mis? . . .] erable self shrunk, cringing before the condemnation of my soul. I tried to hide from it under the blankets; I tried to shut it from my sight with closed eyes. But it stayed and burned and burned until that self was dead. Then came the other vision. At first I dared not look at it. I ran from it. I tried to escape it by shutting out the light and going to bed. But it followed me. Always it was there. A little girl, a little girl as little as a child, sitting on the edge of my prison bed—looking of nowhere into a blank tomorrow, saying a simple thing that was the preamble of a world of love. 'I shall just work and work until I can work no more.' Great God! How it fell upon my breaking spirit. Oh, I could see the damage I had wrought. I could not kiss those sad eyes then. I was unworthy. I was base and low. I feared that majestic declaration of a simple purpose. I tried to escape the crushing indictment of my miserable love that it carried with it. But

I could not. It was long in the morning, in the small hours when at last my cowardly heart faced that last vision; then I began to grow. Then my soul began to reach out and upward—groping for that wonderful soul of yours, drinking as one lost in a desert, of its life-giving strength of purpose and all this tired, worn, racked and broken me, all that was left, fell asleep. It was so sweet to sleep then. I fell asleep all alone. All alone for the first time since I have been here. Always I have gone to sleep on my prison bed with your image in my arms. But last night that would have been profanation. A sacrilege. So I went to sleep alone.

And, oh how wonderful to wake as I did this morning. To feel the kiss of the cool air on my cheek and spring—yes spring from sleep into the light of this new day. Fresh, strong, new, revivified, joy-bringing with every twitching muscle. Oh, sweetheart, the thought of it drives me from my chair. I must get up and pace the jail. Oh but differently now. Yes strength in every stride.

* * *

First, I must answer your letter. I have read it and am reading it again now. Yes, yes, I've read it all over again and you said it will make you happy to know—be happy—be happy—be supremely happy—for I know—I know—I know. When I read some places big things turned over in my breast and rolled up into my throat to choke me while stabs of pain shot thro [sic] my heart and tears welled to my eyes. But I'm happy—as happy as anyone like me can be in a jail. Maybe the letter would have made me see, but I'm rather glad I didn't get it until today. I'm rather glad you did come as you did yesterday and refuse my kiss. I'm glad of all that terrible, nervous, gasping talk of yesterday because it shot all the clouds away. It blew all the wild fancies and vague film wraiths of a slowly decaying mind to atoms and left me this morning with just clear day—blue sky—clean air—high places—unlimited vision—and above all —standing imperious—looking upward to where the light comes from—you—my Galatea—and I there at your feet gazing—gazing just as we both have way back on Charles Island into a western sky, painted in flaming fire at sunset or into a misty dawn breaking with the breaking waves its shadows and fog fading before the clear light of a great golden sun emerging from the seawater. So I saw you this morning—resplendent—divine! Then I knew all—henceforth I will know. Henceforth the madness will not be seen in me. When next you clasp my hand—it will only tremble with pure, clean joy of seeing you. We will tell each other sweet tales of our great love and we will work and strive and live together henceforth—forever more. That is the sum of my suffering. All things up to now have made toward that. All my breakings out in anger—all my storms of the spirit—all my questioning—everything. My last cruel note was the result of hours and hours of brooding over what I thought you had marked in the 'chasm' for us. A mistake, but I give thanks for it. Now, all those things are over.

Well, dear, you must know that in my work in Little Falls a new thing has taken possession of me. I have wondered often whether it was not that new thing that made me so successful in the short time I was there. Wondered whether, now, with that new thing removed I would not be a failure where before I was a success. But I don't think so. The sustaining influence of you won't ever let me fail and even if I did I have the knowledge that it doesn't lose you to me.

You see dear, when I left Bridgeport it was with the bitterest of feelings. I thought you had coldly stepped on me because I was sure you had received my message and once when I passed your house I fancied I saw you draw back from a window to avoid being seen by me. Then I went to the depot. I took the train. Came to Little Falls. Plunged into the fight. I was determined to shut you out of my heart so I took those people in. I took their cause in. Gave everything I had in me to it and got surprising returns. The first day I [missing word(s)] they were spiritless—dead. They had no hope—no courage—no light—no understanding—no desire to fight. They would have slunk back in a week just as they did in Jewett City last spring. They had not understood anyone who spoke to them. They could not follow anyone who tried to lead them. I came to them with a new language. I put all my love for you into words for them to interpret their struggle and I put all that bitterness rankling—that hellish hatred—you call it—into words of scorching fire for their enemies. In two or three days they were transformed. We marched and sang and met together and they grew big and strong. When on Friday, Oct. 25th, I saw for the first time the spirit I had infused in them I think I blotted out the rest of my life. I fed on it. I went on, not rushing, but tactfully playing for the larger sentiment, but feeding the fire. I saw it gathering, but did not think it would break so soon nor the way it did. You know, I was not a ranting orator. I did not shout loudly nor say wild things. I just did things—a rapid succession of sledgehammer blows that left a dent every time. Oh, I am hated in Little Falls, I can tell you, by those who were the marks of my tongue-shafts.

They will cry for blood or fight desperately for years of life to balm their wounded consciences. I could see that coming but went on recklessly—(that is reckless from the point of view of self)—until when they struck and I saw others hurt. Then for the first time in eight days—when I heard a striker had been killed and I felt somehow to blame I began to think of you without the bitterness I had taken away from Bridgeport with me on the train. Now, dear, Felix is here, so more later.

Love interminable and pure for you.

THE LITTLE FALLS EVENING TIMES

AN I.W.W. LOVE LETTER

Copy of a Tender Epistle Sent from this City to a Strike Prisoner in Herkimer Jail:

Herkimer, Feb. 18—Following is a copy of a letter that was found recently, sent to one of the strike prisoners in Herkimer jail. The epistle gives an insight into the workings of the I.W.W. organization and the manner in which it carried on its business. The letter also unfolds a strong love drama that ran along in connection with the textile strike in Little Falls. It was on November 16 that the letter was found and it reads as follows:

511 Jefferson Street,
11:30 p.m.

Sweetheart: My heart just fluttered when I opened your note tonight, and when I read it it eased my aching heart some, for I knew yours ached just a little bit less. It is so hard, dear, to get even a little time off here to write to you, all I do, all I feel my love for you my longing for happiness for us two; the thoughts that storm my brain, the emotions that storm my heart; the many things that I want you to know. Your big sixteen page letter had just a tinge of sarcasm, just enough to make me feel that I was not altogether competent.

Now dear, I want you to have confidence in me for the time that I have been here I did some real good work. Don't forget that I found things smashed up pretty badly and had to do some hustling to get things to even the point at which they are now. The reason I asked for a detailed statement from you was that I am trying hard to get hold of everyone who was in any way concerned with handling stamp book funds, and other things for which I will be responsible. I was elected financial secretary and treasurer as Bakeman could not be here to do this work and then Haywood wants me on the job all the time; I mean even after the strike is settled, for the defense fund. He insisted that I take it and said he couldn't see how the national office can pay me less than organizers wages. So you see my work is appreciated as being valuable. The strike—well, it's a sort of stubborn proposition. The ranks of the strikers are still unbroken, but there is as yet little indication of a speedy settlement. Our picket lines are good, our meetings well attended and enthusiastic; the relief work in proper shape. Meetings have been arranged in several places, and Bill is making efforts to tie the Phoenix branch in Utica. He wants me to tell you not to worry about things outside, altho [*sic*] he says he knows how hard it must be on you to be shut up there with your brain running at such high voltage. Moore promises to be here as soon as he can get away from Salem. Then I believe things will shape themselves quite a bit differently. But Sweetheart, you must not, for my sake and your own, let things sap your vitality to the extent you have. Remember those wonderful lines of Giovannitti's "Rest, sleep, think, my brother for the little key is not the only thing that can throw open the jail doors"; this is as near as I can remember them. By the way, what are you reading and can't I get you some books? or anything, sweetheart everything I have, or can get, is yours. My life, my love, my brain, my hands, all yours, forever—I received everything you have sent me, magazines letters and all. So

did Bill and the others. But I'm so afraid that if you go too strong at it they're apt to cut it off suddenly, and that would be terrible. So be discreet, dear. You know I sent you a note with the candy and other things that night they would not permit me to see you, but I guess they held it, however there was absolutely nothing in it, so much so, that I sent it openly. I suppose the bull heads thought they got something. Did you get the underwear all right, also the two bags of fruit and other things that I sent up? Today we sent a big basket of food, and will send one every day if we know you are getting it. I plead again you must take care of yourself dear, or else I shall be unable to rest, or work, or anything. You must be brave, you must be big and I want you to find some little courage in my hand and always have faith in my heart—never before did I know what you mean to me, and the greatness of my love for you.

But I know now and you shall know too; write me as often as you can but please dear don't put yourself to any more trouble, don't. With boundless love, and a soft sigh that I know will find an echo in your heart, I am yours,

Mat.

The above was written by the young woman who is sending circulars broadcast over the country, appealing for funds and condemning the same officials whom she refers to as "bull heads." Inasmuch as the man to whom the letter was written has a wife and two children, we have here a practical illustration of the working of the free love idea.

Not only were these letters used to prejudice the jury in Ben's trial, they were personally humiliating for Matilda. I think Ben loved the notoriety, and he gave the clippings to me as a point of pride. In spite of embracing unconventional attitudes and ideas, Matilda was modest. The public exposure of her private relationship must have mortified her, hence she disguised the events but could not forget the treachery of the spy (the aforementioned Felix?) that caused so much pain and embarrassment.

After eighty-nine days, the struggle ended in gains, though small, for the workers. The bosses agreed not to discriminate against those mill workers who had been on strike, to reinstate all employees, and to pay every worker, male and female, sixty hours of pay for fifty-four hours of work. On January 3, 1913, at a mass meeting, with Matilda Rabinowitz as chair, the striking workers voted unanimously to accept the settlement offer and agreed to return to work beginning on January 6, just three days before her twenty-sixth birthday. When I want to feel especially close to Matilda, I wear the golden locket the workers gave her, with a picture of baby Vita, my mother, and a lock of hair inside. The outside is engraved: "To Matilda from Little Falls Strikers 1-9-13."

8   A GALLERY OF RADICALS

Saint John, Haywood, Carlo Tresca, John Macy, Phillips Russell, Bob Bakeman, others—a gallery of radicals, liberals, Socialists, justice and freedom seekers—I knew them briefly, yet closely, in the Little Falls strike. In crises, in situations that demand quick thinking, patience, determination, and loyalty to an ideal, personal qualities are revealed. One may see high courage bound to humility, simplicity in deep wisdom, unspoken idealism in everyday relations. One may also find egotism mistaken for courage, pretense parading as idealism, self-seeking masquerading as commanding action. In a crisis, when responsibility is called for, hidden traits in all of us are made manifest.

Who and what were some of these men, women, and events that left such poignant memories, that forever after influenced my thought and action? There was Vincent Saint John, "The Saint," general secretary of the IWW; his letters on organization, his patient explaining of details, his clear, direct eloquently simple language was a true training course through my weeks in Little Falls. He had the skill to cover and make understandable in one paragraph what some of the top organizers and officers took pages to explain far less adequately. From Saint John I learned not only the

basic principles of organization, but some of the art of letter writing. His was a major contribution to my development as an organizer.

Joe Ettor was too busy elsewhere to come to Little Falls. There was a large segment of Italians among the strikers, and at Fred Moore's suggestion, the strike committee asked Carlo Tresca to come. He was said to be an inspirational speaker. Though his English was poor, his Italian was eloquent. He was an impressive-looking figure, tall, handsome, with a flowing tie and a large Stetson hat. Sparkling and affable, Tresca was fascinating. He obviously was aware of the effect he had on people, on audiences, and especially on women. He was entertaining with his garbled English, his generosity and conviviality, but he was little help to us in Little Falls. He gave one or two speeches, but whatever effect he may have had in the union halls of New York City, he fell flat in Little Falls. This was not a dramatic situation involving thousands of strikers. These 1,600 mill workers were dogged, humble strikers unable to appreciate his sophistication. He talked, he ate spaghetti and drank wine, and we paid the bill. When he left I was relieved and greatly disappointed.

Later, I revealed my disappointment to Fred Moore and Phillips Russell. Moore loved the eloquence of Tresca but had to admit it had

served us poorly in Little Falls. Russell, a keener critic, while liking Tresca, suggested that mere speech-making was futile in the absence of organizational ability.

Russell himself was doing an excellent job at absurdly low pay, because he was attuned to the meaning and demands of the struggle. Though he later divorced himself from the radical movement, and wrote a number of biographies of famous Americans (Franklin, Emerson), I always remembered him for his integrity, tolerance, and respect for the struggles of the workers.

John Macy, a journalist and writer on social problems, the husband of Anne Sullivan (teacher of Helen Keller), was humble in his desire to help. He assisted with the accounting, printed signs, typed our leaflets, and marched in our picket line. A friendly, humorous, gracious man, he came for a few days and left behind him a warm glow of sympathy and understanding of the need for a reconstructed social order.

Most dedicated to the idea of a just social order was Bob Bakeman, an ex-minister. He took the teachings of Jesus literally and could not accept the inconsistencies and hypocrisy of institutionalized religion. He gave up his church, embraced Socialism, helped wherever

possible in workers' organizations, and brought a crusader's spirit to every strike. He was young and eloquent and joyous, as if drawing the very essence of his being from his identity with the poor, the exploited, and the persecuted.

Of course, he was ostracized by his denomination and by former friends and associates. He was a source of grief to his family, especially his father who loved him and had had great hopes of success for him, and he felt this alienation keenly. How moved I was when he

sang, "I am a stranger here upon a foreign land / My home is far away...," and yet he glowed with the recognition of his need to serve, to give all he had. His father was a prominent minister, and once he showed me a letter from him. It was a sad letter, the letter of a disappointed father who feared his son's activities and the danger to which he exposed himself "in a foreign land." He was especially fearful of the IWW, and the letter was signed, "your affectionate father, until you join the IWW." Bob made a joke about the conditions for affection, but the old man did not really mean it that way. I don't think Bob Bakeman ever joined the IWW, but neither did he return to his father's "foreign land." Bob was a rare spirit, a man committed above all else to the ideal he lived by—the brotherhood of man. How I envied and admired him!

From Little Falls I carried away an increased sense of responsibility to the IWW, but I had a great reluctance at the same time of becoming a professional organizer. Some money was coming in, and I kept the accounts and was charged with the running expenditures of the strike, but there was no financial arrangement between me and the organization. I went to Little Falls at my own expense and had about forty dollars when I got there. When this was gone I didn't know how I was going to get along. I paid room rent to the striker's family where I was living, ate at least one meal in a restaurant, and there were incidental personal expenses: laundry and carfare, for example. I received no money from the national office and I did not know that the local organization was meant to assume my expenses while I was there. It was not until Bill Haywood arrived and I told him of my precarious situation that the minimum for living expenses was allowed me by the strike committee. Later I was to become a national organizer for the Textile Workers Industrial Union and would receive $18 a week, when there was money in the treasury.

AGAIN, WHERE ARE THE WOMEN? JAILED along with Ben and Bob Bakeman, whose spirit and commitment impress, Helen Schloss merits no mention. Helen Keller's letter to the strikers of Little Falls was important in gathering outside support for the strike, as well as inspiring to the strikers. Matilda describes Keller's friend and mentor John Macy—his humility and helpful support—without noting Keller's contribution. Keller wrote to the strike committee:

I am sending the check which Mr. Davis paid me for the Christmas sentiments I sent him. Will you give it to the brave girls who are striving so courageously to bring about the emancipation of the workers at Little Falls? They have my warmest sympathy. Their cause is my cause. If they are denied a living wage, I also am denied. While they are industrial slaves, I cannot be free. My hunger is not satisfied while they are unfed. I cannot enjoy the good things of life which come to me, if they are hindered and neglected, I want all the workers of the world to have sufficient money to provide the elements of a normal standard of living—a decent home, healthful surroundings, opportunity for education and recreation. I want them all to have the same blessings that I have. I, deaf and blind, have been helped to overcome many obstacles. I want them to be helped as generously in a struggle which resembles my own in many ways.*

Although she was attracted to the work and committed to the struggle, Matilda expresses reluctance to continue as an organizer and suggests that the precarious pay was an issue. As direct as she could be when seeking help on her own behalf from the WTUL, she didn't ask about financial support from the IWW national office. Only after she mentioned her financial worries to Haywood was she offered the position of a paid organizer.

Matilda remembers expenditures with specificity. From the very beginning of her story, she guesses the Ukrainian nanny's wage. She remembers the cost of a potted geranium in New York in 1900, what a gross of finished ties netted, the fee for the tutor she engaged to prepare her for college, every wage she was paid, the cost of a room, a meal, her father's wages, and her salary as an IWW organizer—$18.00 a week "when there was money in the treasury."

In our family she was known to be careful with money, good at budgeting, and vigilant about expenses. She feared debt (as did her

---

*Helen Keller, *Helen Keller: Her Socialist Years*, ed. Phillip S. Foner (New York: International Publishers, 1968), 12–14, 32–35.

mother). She was valuable as an organizer because, among other qualities, she was a conscientious bookkeeper. She recognized value but was modest in her needs and wants. She always bought at sales and bargained for services. She worried about money but always managed.

She opposed the convention of tipping, believing that workers should be paid fairly for their services and not have to rely on gratuities. It embarrassed me when we went to a restaurant and she didn't tip. However, when at seventeen I was a waitress at the Mayfair lunch counter in Fresno, she came in and ordered an ice cream sundae, which might have cost fifty cents. When she left and I cleared away the dishes, there was a silver dollar under the saucer. I was astonished. This was one of very few examples of Matilda's principles giving way to affection. My hourly wage was less than the tip she left.

9 AFTER LITTLE FALLS

The Légère-Bocchini Defense Committee was stillborn. The national office of the IWW would carry on the defense by retaining Fred Moore as counsel, as in the beginning, but nothing was contemplated like the agitation which followed the Lawrence strike and the Ettor-Giovannitti case. Little Falls was more remote from the center of the textile industry, the case not likely to draw much publicity, and the two men connected with the case were little known, even to the strikers. Then there was Paterson, which at its height in the winter of 1913 absorbed the attention of IWW leaders, radical writers, intelligentsia, volunteers, and liberals close to the scene in and around New York City. There were several smaller strikes going on throughout New England, and urgent appeals for organizers coming into the national office, but at the same time membership in Lawrence after the dramatic strike and defense of the leaders was dwindling seriously until it was down to a mere few hundred paying dues. Strikes do not bring in money to national unions; strikes take and use money. The IWW strikes were mainly self-supporting.

On my way from Little Falls I stopped in New York briefly, where I met Saint John for the first time. He was there only briefly. Haywood, Flynn, and Tresca were in the headlines and in the public eye. There were, as always, scores of others who formed the backbone of the strike, who were driven from place to place by the police, who were

149

arrested, given jail and prison sentences, and their names are too numerous to list. But in the work and the endurance of the strikers lie the outcome of all strikes. I do not disparage leadership, but it is too often merely window dressing, a volatile agent for self-consciousness.

I went over to Paterson with Flynn and Tresca, and things seemed quiet that evening. They took me to dinner—Italian food, of course. Tresca, always the connoisseur, was convivial as usual. The man loved his food and his wine. And in his quaint, flamboyant English he outtalked everybody. I had a feeling that Flynn, prominent, even famous as she was, was in awe of him. His leaving her was a great tragedy for her. For him, another love, continuous agitation against Mussolini, and a tragic death in 1944 when he was shot down on a New York street.

The National Office reached me in New York and directed me to a strike in Shelton, Connecticut, where a strike had broken out in the [Sidney] Blumenthal Mills. Here, broad silk and some of the most beautiful ribbons were being woven. Several hundred workers, mostly French-Canadian, with smaller groups of Russians and Germans, were resisting a cut in wages and a shorter workday. The pattern, as I found it in the textile workers' strikes that I participated in, was much the same everywhere: low pay, long hours, speed-up, slack, reduction of wages.

I spent seven weeks, during February and March, in Shelton. The winter was a severe one. There was the usual grim endurance of the strikers, the resistance to their organization by the employers, the small gains at the end. The pattern for the organizer is also largely repetitious—to lay the groundwork for a union, to develop the meaning of economic solidarity, to organize relief, to publicize the strike, to assume various and innumerable administrative details. The daily picket line, the nightly meeting, the reports, the negotiations, at last. In the small strike the organizer, not merely a speaker, is both administrator and teacher. I considered my assignment, whether in a strike or out, as an organizing job. Speaking seemed the least important part.

The intimate contacts, the administrative detail in a community of striking workers, the collective enterprise minus any profit motive, the instruction of others who would remain after the organizer had departed, these were of greater importance. The failure of the IWW to hold an organization was due in large part to lack of such capabilities on the part of its organizers.

Shelton was no more and no less a severe struggle in midwinter than Little Falls, than half a dozen other small strikes in which I had assignments in 1913. The gains by the strikers were always too small for the endurance put forth. But something beyond the small material gain was left from every strike, from every effort of workers to band together to resist their condition of work and of living. Certainly we of the IWW with our concept of a Socialist society and a program of revolutionary unionism knew that beyond the pennies an hour more, and the reduced workday won, the worker must aspire to something more, must grasp the meaning of his place in society. And we bore proudly the slogan: "Education, Organization, Emancipation."

Following Shelton I did some organizing for the IWW among pottery workers in East Liverpool, Ohio, as well as speaking in Youngstown, Toledo, and Akron.

Although I was officially an organizer for the Textile Workers Industrial Union, the national office often asked me to take on assignments in other industries. There were never enough organizers, and women organizers were still a novelty. I could mount a soapbox in a pinch, so the summer found me in Detroit, where the IWW was active

Matilda Radnowitz On Way to Jail

in the Studebaker strike. It was June 1913 and some 5,000 were out on strike. There were some 50–60,000 auto workers in Detroit at the time. There was little organization, and the IWW local was weak, having neither the expertise nor even a clear understanding of the magnitude of the job to be done. Although it had a group of excellent speakers, they were not organizers with plans and discipline enough to tackle the job. They carried on much agitation from soapboxes at the factory gates, not only at Studebaker, but also at Ford and other automobile plants. There were arrests and harassment by the police. Speakers were pulled off soapboxes, arrested, and jailed overnight, just long enough to dis-

rupt meetings, then released the following day. Usually the cases against them were dismissed. I was arrested at Ford in Highland Park and jailed for one night. In court, the arresting officer towered above me. The charge? "Obstructing traffic," he told the judge. I pleaded not guilty, and the case was dismissed. This kind of harassment was typical. Without organization and planning, the strike dissipated itself. Many years were to elapse before the auto workers would move as a mass toward industrial unionism.

Following Detroit I was sent to the Pittsburgh area in the summer of 1913. Several hundred stogie-makers had been out several weeks. The strikers, mostly women and teenaged girls, made 11–14 cents to make a hundred stogies. These were the cheapest cigars, known as three for or even four for (three or four for a nickel). The demand

was for 12–15 cents per hundred. Through the summer and fall I covered Pittsburgh, Philadelphia, and McKeesport where the IWW was carrying on active organization among transport and steel workers. As the only woman known here among the IWW organizers, I was something of a curiosity. My soapboxing drew considerable publicity and a bit too much for the authorities in McKeesport. I was arrested and sentenced to 30 days in jail or a fine of $50, again for obstructing traffic. Of course, the only traffic where I had been speaking was steel workers on the way home from a 12-hour shift. My soapbox was in the center of unpaved, rutty streets that led to the grimy shacks of the steel workers, and my arrest was, of course, merely police harassment. IWWs were not paying fines in those days, and so to the Western Pennsylvania penitentiary I went.

Prison did not seem too terrible. Conditions were no better and no worse than in most of the prisons of that day. The food was poor, the bunk was hard, sanitation was primitive, but the nightly crying and cursing of the women in the adjacent cells was dreadful. There was some relief during the day in the light and airy rooms where we made shirts and other garments for male prisoners, but the silence system prevailed. Eight hours of total silence even though one was in the company of many was hard to bear. The Wobbly boys, although many of them had been in and out of jail many times, couldn't bear the thought of me being in prison, so after 12 days they paid my fine. I was released.

As a national organizer on assignment to raise strike and defense funds, I was again sent to Ohio. In March 1914, I was in Akron where rubber workers were on strike. This was a fierce battle and another losing one. However, it was here that I saw for the first time the IWW and Socialists work extremely well together. In the home of militant Socialists Frank and Margaret Prevey, the organizers and speakers from the IWW made their headquarters.

The Preveys were opticians, comfortably off and devoted to the cause of Socialism. Margaret was a lifelong and devoted friend of Eugene Debs, serving him and the movement in triumph and adversity. A handsome, warm, energetic woman she dispensed hospitality that knew no bounds and was a person to admire, to respect, and to love. I stayed in the Prevey home during the two weeks I spent in the strike. There I came to know Mary Marcy, her husband Leslie, who was doing some of the publicity for the strike, William Trautmann, one of the founders of the IWW, Jim Cannon, organizer, later a Communist, then a Trotskyist and leader of Trotsky orthodoxy in America, and George Speed, the brilliant editor of the *International Socialist Review.*

George Speed was the incarnation of the complete proletarian revolutionist. He knew no life outside the IWW, but he rebelled against the intolerable conditions of the seaman long before the IWW was born. For fifty years or more, as agitator and organizer, he commuted between the Atlantic and Pacific coasts, stopping at intermediate transport and shipping points, agitating and organizing, organizing

and agitating. To his fellow seamen he spoke of a
world that would replace their condition of slavery with decency, dignity, education, a better livelihood, and eventually emancipation. More than
anyone in the IWW, speaker, writer, or organizer,
George Speed made me believe in the precept of
the IWW preamble: "It is the historic mission of
the working class to abolish capitalism." He stood
tall and straight and weather-beaten. He was utterly selfless. I remember him sitting in front of the
fire in the Prevey home, talking in a slow drawl,
his eyes half-shut, relaxed. We younger people
sometimes listened and sometimes were preoccu-
pied with each other. George Speed died at 70 in a
county hospital in the Pacific Northwest. For me

he was a symbol of the best, the noblest in a proletarian revolutionist.

Mary Marcy was feminine and tragic. She was considered one of
the most intellectual women of the Socialist movement in the United States. She was certainly the best informed, and a gifted writer.
The *International Socialist Review*, where she was editor, was the most
revolutionary Socialist journal in the country. She was also top editor at Charles H. Kerr Publishers, where practically all American
Socialist literature was published. During the evenings that she was
with our group, she appeared tense, quiet, and almost timid before
her husband, Leslie. He was jolly, bubbling over with friendliness,
most likeable. Mary seemed to follow him everywhere with her eyes.
I heard later that she was deeply and unhappily in love with him and
suffered from his reported philandering. I did not know it at the time,
but I wondered at her gay attire and the sadness of her face. Eight
years later Mary Marcy committed suicide. Disillusionment, it was
said. Of what?—the Socialist movement in America during World
War I and after? Desertion of American Socialists? The flight of Bill
Haywood to Russia? (Mary's house had been mortgaged to help raise

the $40,000 bail which Haywood jumped.) Most people said the Haywood business was the final blow which drove her over the edge of despair, but who can fathom the cause of suicide?

The Akron strike dragged and it sagged and it expired with attrition. Early thaws and floods in Akron added to the distraction and discomfort of the strikers. They drifted back to work, disorganized and defeated. It would be many years before the seeds dropped by the IWW would germinate and the rubber workers of Akron would revolt.

AFTER MATILDA'S BRIEF VISIT TO PATERSON AND DINNER with Flynn, Tresca, and Haywood, she was sent to Shelton to help organize a much smaller, less significant Wobbly strike of silk weavers.

Paterson, a major center of silk weaving in the United States since the prior century, had about three hundred mills where both ribbon and broad silk were loomed. The majority of the workers were men, who in contrast to other textile workers were considered highly skilled, because the delicate thread was difficult to weave. Thus they were better paid than the less skilled workers in Lawrence and Little Falls. Silk mills had been more recently mechanized than other textile industries. This strike differed from Lawrence and Little Falls in that wages were not the primary issue, but working conditions and hours were. The workers' main complaint was that new mechanization obliged them to operate three or four looms at a time, rather than the one or two they formerly worked, and made it possible for the factory to employ half as many workers. The silk weavers also agitated for the eight-hour workday.

The Paterson strike was long and bitter. An IWW local had been formed there prior to the walkout, and the national office sent their stars to help. As she had in Lawrence, Flynn organized an exodus of the strikers' children to be cared for outside of Paterson, and the strike also became a cause célèbre for Socialists and Greenwich Village bohemians—artists and writers. The journalist John Reed (the author of *Ten Days that Shook the World*, about the Russian Revolution) organized a pageant about the strike, the artist John Sloan contributed paintings for the set, and many Greenwich Village writers were involved as well. Although the pageant filled Madison Square Garden, it was not a financial success. Not only did it not raise money for the strike, it lost money. After six months of struggle the strikers went back to work without winning any concessions.

Shelton, Connecticut, did not attract Wobbly luminaries, as Paterson or Lawrence had. Matilda blames the organizers' lack of administrative abilities and their unwillingness to mentor the strikers for the IWW's failure to maintain a presence in these small strikes. Implicit in her comment that fiery speeches are less important than educating and attending to administrative details is a severe appraisal of her dining companions, Flynn, Tresca, and Haywood, all riveting orators. But Matilda made an impression in Shelton.

An article from *The Bridgeport Evening Farmer*, January 3, 1914, describes the funeral for an infant who died of starvation and exposure, having been left alone in the house from which her parents, Shelton strikers, were removed by O'Brien's agents.* That agency, similar to the Pinkertons, was a private, militarized police force hired by the industrialists to break up strikes and dispatch strikers. In the newspaper article Matilda is described as "Shelton's Joan of Arc" walking near the front of the funeral cortège.

The brevity of Matilda's description of Detroit surprises me, because she is better known for her efforts there than in strikes that she found much more grueling. Automation was new to the industry in 1913 (her father in Bridgeport was still working at Locomobile, a plant that built cars by hand). The very first auto industry strike was the one Matilda organized at Studebaker. She then urged the workers on to the Packard plant to build the momentum for an industry-wide shutdown. Henry Ford's Model T assembly shop was next door. Some blame Matilda for Henry Ford's decision to offer his employees $5.00 a day (considered generous at the time) in order to divert workers' attempts to unionize. The importance of this strike is reflected in the notice paid to her leadership by historians, both professional and amateur.

I met one of the latter when I searched for her in Detroit. It was the first time I had been to Motown, and I wanted to see her papers, and Ben's, in the labor archives of the Walter Reuther Library at Wayne State University. Terry Judd, whom I met through a query I received from him on the Internet, had discovered the Detroit Public Library's newspaper article files about Matilda's organizing and arrest. When I visited, he offered to show me "Matilda's Detroit." He knew where the Studebaker plant had been and showed me the decaying, derelict Packard factory where she had marched with the workers. She was arrested as she addressed the workers leaving Studebaker for their lunch break. Terry discovered photos in the Detroit Public Library archives that portrayed Matilda's arrest along with those of others. She

---

*CT, "The Joan of Arc of Shelton, the Efficiency Man, the O'Briens, and Sidney Blumenthal," Connecticut Digital Newspaper Project, December 30, 2015, http:// ctdigitalnewspaperproject.org/2015/12/the-joan-of-arc-of-shelton-the-efficiency-man-the-obriens-and-sidney-blumenthal/.

dismissed the arrest as mere harassment: the charge was obstructing traffic, and the case was dismissed.

An article found by Terry Judd contradicts Matilda's memory. The *Detroit Free Press*, April 29, 1913, says that Matilda and three other Wobblies, three men, were fined $5.00 each for obstructing traffic and describes her (with an approximation of her actual surname) as follows:

Matilda Radnowitz [*sic*] mounted the box. She is short and very attractive in appearance. She is of the Russian type of beauty, having come from the land of the czar 12 years ago. The appearance of this diminutive organizer seemed out of place in the throng of men in overalls with faces soiled after a morning's work in the shop. She seemed to be the leader of the organizers.

Later the article says:

Miss Radnowitz participated in the strike of textile workers at Little Falls, N.Y., where 1500 women went out. She was also prominent in the rubber workers strike at Akron O. where 17000 men and women stayed out seven weeks. Six weeks ago she was arrested in East Liverpool, O., while addressing 700 girls who worked in potteries. She is 25 years old.

She was actually 26. The paper provides her address: 66 Milwaukee Ave. I looked for this address on Google, but evidently the building that bore that address, like so many in today's Detroit, has disappeared.

If she even read the article or saw the accompanying pictures of the arrest, she doesn't say. "There were never enough organizers, and women organizers were still a novelty," she writes, and the press obviously was fascinated. She saved no clippings. No doubt she found the press report trivial and condescending—"Russian beauty," indeed!

10 GREENVILLE, SOUTH CAROLINA, "THE TOUGHEST JOB"

It was the spring of 1914, and I was 27 years old. My family still lived in Bridgeport, and my father was still working at the Locomobile plant. David, the eldest brother, to whom I was very close, had given up his newspaper stand to a younger brother, Morris. Samuel, now 23, was working in the Remington arms plant. My beloved only sister, Minnie, 19, had completed a business course and had become a stenographer. The two youngest ones, Herman and Bob, were still in school. But with so many working, there was a little more income in the family—a piano and better clothing. Although she was generally a good housekeeper, my mother never learned to cook properly for the family. Her meals were heavy with fat and starch, and she served few vegetables, never fresh vegetables or fruits.

My visit home that spring was anything but reassuring to my parents. I remained unmarried. I floated about the country in this strange business of organizing workers. I was rootless. They grieved over the turn my life had taken, but for me there was no turning back. Only David understood my drive. He had educated himself in the same way I did and had wanted to be a journalist. Although he took various jobs in publicity, advertising, or other odd writing jobs, he never found himself in any consistent occupation. He married late, past 30, to a schoolteacher. Their marriage was not happy. Frances was a practical, conventional person, and she resented David's hapless occupations which brought in very little money. She continued teaching and largely made the family living. They had two boys, Richard and Eugene, and when they were 10 and 12 years old David and Frances divorced.

My few weeks at home were difficult. The family ties had never been very strong, and now they were permanently broken. I always visited the family between organizing jobs but never again lived at home.

In the late spring of 1914 I was assigned to the job of organizing textile workers in the South Carolina mills. This was my first visit to the South and the beginning of a new kind of organizing experience.

Greenville, South Carolina, was then a town of about 32,000 with a mill population of 16,000. Within a radius of 20 or 30 miles around Greenville were scattered a number of small mills. It was a territory untouched by any organization. I found conditions there which were typical of mill workers' conditions prevalent in the South: company-owned shacks with outdoor privies, a hydrant every third house, wretched oil stoves for cooking, smoky fireplaces, unplastered walls, and one dim 25 watt light swinging from a ceiling cord. The whole family worked in the mill. Men earned about a dollar a day, women 90 cents, children less. There was no age limit, and I saw children as young as nine or ten working as little duffer boys and girls. And there were boys and girls of 14 who could not remember how many years they had worked in the mills. The workday was 12 hours—from 6 a.m. to 6 p.m.

With these low wages, it is easy to imagine the standard of living of these exploited workers. Fat pork, grits, hominy, corn bread, and something the company store sold as coffee was the unvarying fare. There were no green vegetables, no fresh fruit, no fresh milk on the table, ever. The southeastern European workers in the New England mills ate a lot of cabbage, the Italians leafy greens along with their spaghetti—some variety, at least. The diet of the Southern workers was appalling to me.

I stayed with a mill family at first and shared their crowded quarters and meager food. They were friendly and helpful and pleased to have the organizer sharing their home. Later I found a room in the home of a poor middle-class family, where I could have a bath and a fairly comfortable bed and a table for my work with a good light. The Webbs, like thousands of their class, were holding on to their old home and old traditions. Mr. Webb had some sort of office job with the railroad, poorly paid, obviously, or they would not have needed

the ten dollars per month I paid for my room. Mrs. Webb was an attractive woman in her early thirties, educated in a small denominational women's college. She was reserved, yet friendly. They had five children, all under the age of ten. I took my meals in a restaurant run by a Greek.

When I rented the room, which had been advertised in the local paper, I told Mrs. Webb that I was a labor organizer and in Greenville to organize textile workers. She looked surprised, but there were no questions, and she accepted me. During my ten weeks there she learned more about my work, saw the IWW and other literature in my room, but never suggested that I was in any way objectionable to her. It was I who was surprised, first by being taken in at all, and then by the unfailing friendliness she showed to me.

She was a busy woman with a large house and, besides the children, an aged aunt who demanded attention. I talked with Mrs. Webb now and then about my work and the mill workers. They were strangers to her; she knew nothing of that part of her town, but she showed interest and sympathy. Mr. Webb I hardly ever saw. He seemed dour and dull, and from the little she said I gathered that he disapproved of me and of the mill workers.

It was the toughest job in my entire organizing career, but the groundwork was laid. Small, old mills were being supplanted by modern big ones, and rural families were being brought to the mill towns and rapidly made into machine tenders. There were few skilled workers, but even these had never been approached by the craft-minded American Federation of Labor. I suppose they did not consider there were enough of them to bother with. The idea of organizing into a union was completely new to these people, and to the bosses it was ludicrous.

Ben and Bocchini were tried, convicted, and sentenced to a year in the Auburn penitentiary. I read of the trial and sentence but could not bring myself to write to Ben. We had had no contact for more than a year, but I managed to torment myself with thoughts of him. I cannot say exactly why I left Greenville after six weeks of intensive organization. I had established a local, and perhaps a hundred workers joined. Very likely I wanted some respite from the task and hoped to persuade another organizer to go down.

I returned to Bridgeport and then to New York where I stayed temporarily with Joe Ettor's wife, Iva Shuster. It was in her apartment where I met Ben again. He had been discharged from prison some months before, but he was not doing anything. He had expected to be more recognized, to be given speaking dates, to be assigned organizing jobs by the IWW, but the organization did not call him. He drifted between Bridgeport and New York, trying to attach himself to the stage. He went around to agencies with the play he had written years before, and he had a few months' work as a reader for Universal Films which had offices then in New York. Relatives in Bridgeport took care of his three children, and their mother worked some. He got along somehow and seemed to be enjoying bohemian radicalism. How he got along I was to know later.

When we met there was a pang—recognition of the old love. I kept telling myself that it could never be. In August, just before the war in Europe started, I left again for South Carolina.

My return sparked activity. Both workers and bosses became aware that this business of unionism was serious, and now the bosses did not think it so ludicrous anymore. The newspaper took up the cry of "invaders from the North" come to disturb the tranquility of the South. The workers were warned against the outsiders. Revival meetings in tents near the mills were calling on the mill workers to stay away from the union hall and come to Jesus. But the workers came to the nightly meetings. They had heard the preachers before. The union was something real. They liked the Wobbly song "Pie in the Sky."

The bosses thought it was real, too. Someone remembered something. Someone remembered the staid and respectable AFL. There was a craft here and there in Greenville. One day the newspaper reported that a Mrs. Sara Conboy, an official of the United Textile Workers (AFL), was in town with plans to form a local. She was said to be seeing some tool fixers and foremen and was being taken round the town in a superintendent's car. I got reports from some of the members of the local that she had been taken through the mills by the bosses. They described her as a fat lady in fancy clothes.

Insofar as I knew she never held a meeting with mill workers; none were ever announced in the local newspaper, nor had any of our members been solicited. Whether or not she tried to make some arrangements with the bosses and didn't succeed, or whether the task was too great and the pickings too slim for the union lady from Boston, I could not tell, but she left in a few days and nothing was ever heard from the UTW.

I remained for over three months. It was uphill work, but the workers were learning. The local was slowly growing, and the members
were beginning to talk of making demands for wage increases and a
shorter work week. I was beginning to feel the strain of the work and
asked the national office to relieve me, at least temporarily. No one
was available. I finally decided to leave to make a personal report and
stress the urgency of the situation.

In New York I talked to Joe Ettor, who was then general organizer,
and I urged him to replace me immediately. Still there was no one
available. Soon the news came in that the local was in desperate need
of guidance, that the possibility of a strike was looming. Then Ettor
himself went to Greenville. He remained there just a few days. He did
not think the situation warranted a longer stay. He cautioned against

a precipitate strike and promised to send another organizer. He pressed me to return. But I was too exhausted by
the twenty weeks previous to undertake more immediately. I also felt that Joe preferred the platform of the
large industrial centers to the squalid isolation of the
hinterland. Greenville was a long way from New York
and even from the smaller [northeastern] towns where
an organizer could find kindred spirits and relax around
a bottle of red wine and spaghetti. South Carolina was an
alien land, an extremely difficult organizational terrain. The
ability to assess the raw material was necessary; the willingness to
stay long enough to teach the native workers the elementary principles and methods of unionism was essential. Organizing the Southern textile workers was a long project and would mean often unremit-
ting labor. Joe did not go down to Greenville again, and the general
office apparently could find no one else to go. The work lapsed. Soon
the Greenville local disintegrated, and the IWW abandoned the
Southern textile field, leaving the scattered beginning for other organizations to bring to life years later. It was a sad lesson for me. It was
my last tour of duty as national organizer for the IWW. After 1916 I
undertook no assignments.

"THIS WAS THE BEGINNING OF A NEW KIND OF
organizing experience."

"My few weeks at home were difficult. The family ties had never
been very strong, and now they were permanently broken. I always
visited the family between organizing jobs but never again lived at
home."

Matilda offers little glimpses of her difficult relationship with her
mother throughout the memoir. Her earliest critique touches on her
mother's lack of education. Apparently Bertha was functionally illiterate and learned no language but Yiddish. Matilda treasured her

own literacy and facility for languages and was sometimes contemptuous of her mother's character and temperament. She describes her parents' marriage as unhappy, and she appears to be more sympathetic to her father. What Bertha sees as her husband's failings seem almost commendable to Matilda. She belittles her mother's petit bourgeois aspirations, her attempts to start a small business—a candy shop, a grocery. In contrast, Matilda seems to approve of her father's indifference to commerce and his finding respite in intellectual pursuits—sitting with a glass of tea and the paper or conversing with friends. Jacob had been educated for the rabbinate but became an atheist. However, he relished the Jewish tradition of ethical discourse and argument about law and the meaning of the religious cannon.

She is silent about her feelings during the weeks at home between organizing tasks. There must have been friction between Matilda and her mother, who was undoubtedly disappointed and critical. Matilda grudgingly acknowledges her mother's housekeeping skills but can't resist criticizing her cooking as nutritionally inadequate. Elsewhere, too, she responds to her disapproval by offering examples of her mother's ignorance and other failures.

Although Matilda adored her little sister, Minnie, her brother David seems to be the only family member who understood her. In her short descriptions of David, as in those of her father, she shows acceptance bordering on approval of his ineffectual pursuit of material success. Like their parents', David's marriage was unhappy, but his, unlike theirs, ended in divorce. Eugene, David's oldest child, committed suicide in his early twenties, and the younger, Richard, is the only member of Matilda's extended family I ever knew. My mother was very close to that cousin; others she barely knew.

"I cannot say exactly why I left Greenville after six weeks of intensive organization. I had established a local, and perhaps a hundred workers joined. Very likely I wanted some respite from the task and hoped to persuade another organizer to go down," Matilda says.

Besides the loneliness, isolation, and magnitude of the task, there is another possible explanation to the mystery of Matilda's leaving with the job unfinished. When I looked for information about organizing the cotton mills of the south, I came across a pamphlet, *Southern Cotton Mills and Labor*, published by the Workers Library and written by Myra Page in 1929.*

Apparently, the Communist Party sent Page to organize workers in the mills surrounding Greenville. This paragraph from the pamphlet is striking:

> The story followed, one I heard often on the hill, since they were sure I was not spying for the company. During the war "th' I.W.W had come." A woman organizer . . . posted bills, made fiery speeches, and pleased and frightened their souls by the evil things she said of the company. Everybody was for joining the union. The news spread to all the villages that someone had come to help them at last, and there were spontaneous strikes with nobody to lead them. . . . Over here on Huchins hill, they had 85 per cent joined up and had secret meetings with the organizer. Then as they found out afterwards, a company tool got himself elected secretary and everything started going wrong. Right away the workers took to quarreling among themselves. One night a bunch of rowdies, hired by the company, came from another hill and threw rotten eggs and stones at the organizer and drove her out of town, and threatened her ever come back. She did come back, once, and held another secret meeting but it looked like things was all wrong by then. And that was the end of the union.

The woman had to be Matilda; the IWW had no other women organizers at this time except Elizabeth Gurley Flynn, and if she had organized in Greenville during World War I, she surely would have described it in her memoir. I imagine the attack, if it occurred, terrified my grandmother. It must have been humiliating, as well, some-

*https://archive.org/details/SouthernCottonMillsAndLabor.

thing she wanted to forget and keep to herself. Matilda doesn't mention secret meetings and, in fact, writes that she was open about her activities with her landlady, Mrs. Webb.

Flynn had initiated the practice of holding separate meetings for women as a way of encouraging them to organize and assert their communal strength. The meetings Matilda organized helped her to understand the full measure of misery that was these women's lives—grinding work in the mills followed by the duties of wife and mother burdened by serial pregnancies, poverty, prejudice, and ignorance.

Did the news of Ben's release from prison, and an opportunity to connect with him again, hasten her return to New York? And why, after what she must have been through, did she return to Greenville to try again? Her description of Sara Conboy being taken around to the mills in the superintendent's car is an ironic comparison with the IWW's approach to organizing. I imagine the "fat lady in fancy clothes" in contrast to Matilda. Petite, dark, simply attired, and unaccompanied, she carried on the struggle for twenty lonely, difficult weeks.

Matilda is both angry and sad to see the education, encouragement, and organization she initiated come to nothing, after struggling alone for so long. Ettor's visit to Greenville, his dismissal of the possibility of a strike, and his quick departure back to the good food, abundant wine, and conviviality of New York disappointed her. She described a character modeled on Ettor in a fictional fragment and also wrote of an actual sad encounter with him when they met at his wife's funeral. In all her writing about him she reveals disappointment tinged with contempt for his abandoning the IWW when it most needed organizational support. She must have felt especially devastated that the IWW allowed the work to lapse after all she did in Greenville preparing the ground. Her friendship with Ettor's wife, Iva Schuster, continued though, until Iva's death.

Years later the Communist Party, as well as labor unions such as the AFL, made attempts to fill the void left when the IWW abandoned the field. Although Matilda doesn't say so, those traumatic events, if they happened to her, would have been a significant reason for her withdrawal from Greenville and an end to her life as an organizer. After Greenville, Matilda's concerns turned toward survival strategies for herself and her daughter.

11 NEW YORK, GREENWICH, WORLD WAR I

I needed a job. But what should I do? I had left the corset factories in Connecticut. The temporary appointments I had with the industrial investigations could not lead to anything permanent, as I was not eligible for civil service. I was now living in New York temporarily sharing Iva Shuster's apartment on Charles Street. Iva suggested that I learn typing and shorthand and become an office worker. There was the typewriter, she said and the *Gregg Shorthand Manual*, and anyone with my intelligence and enough discipline should learn basic shorthand in six weeks and touch typing in one month. She herself was entirely self-tutored and was one of Gregg's crack shorthand writers. She was now a court reporter. It was a challenge and I met it.

While I was staying with Iva, Ben turned up. "He stayed for hours," she told me, "and talked constantly—all about Ben, until I had to ask him to leave, as I was cramming for a stiff examination." Ben came back when I was there and then again and again. I left New York and went to Greenwich, Connecticut, where I first had a short job as stenographer and then with a weekly, *Our Town*, where I did a variety of office and editorial work. I was getting $12 a week and had cheap living quarters near the office over an interior decorator's shop.

Ben came by again and again, and soon our old relationship was resumed. He lived in New York in a furnished room. Unemployed, he haunted the theatrical agencies and spent the rest of the time seeing plays on courtesy tickets. He offered to review plays for *Our Town*. That meant free tickets to the theater. And so for many weeks of the theatrical season Ben was in his glory as a first-nighter. Some weekends he spent with me, but in the fall of 1916, I left *Our Town*, since the paper could not afford even my small pay, and I went to New York to look for work. For a short time I did some space work for the *New York Tribune* on women in industry. Later, I took a job as stenographer with the Guaranty Trust Company at $125 a month. The war in Europe created increased demand for workers. Wages went up, and bonuses were offered. I was with the GTC when the Russian revolution broke out. When the Kerensky government was set up the GTC was preparing to send a staff to Petrograd to establish a branch. My knowledge of Russian took me out of the stenographic personnel and set me to work on translation and looking up Russian banking laws. Among the thousand or so employees of the bank, people with a knowledge of Russian were at a premium, so I became an important person.

These were exciting days, and the various departments of this second largest bank in the USA were in a frenzy of activity. Now there was a drive for exploitation of this great land that had always been too difficult and inaccessible for trade and commerce. Ancient laws and restrictions had made it all but impossible, but now, with the new regime, it was expected that there would be liberalization and much business.

I listened to the droning of stock and bonds prices (my desk was in the Bond Department), watched the scurrying of clerks, the orders of executives, the tense atmosphere inside and outside the bank and on Wall Street, and as a Socialist I saw the truth of the axiom that "war is the health of the state." This was the time in my life that I could have returned to Russia, but for a bank? I couldn't. I was too much of a Socialist for that, but I had stayed there for six months.

I had an apartment on 23rd Street near Ninth Avenue. Ben was still looking for the elusive theater job. He had a coterie of bohemian friends, mostly unemployed and mostly supported by wives and sweethearts. The Irish revolutionary movement, Sinn Féin, was active then. A number of young Irish-Americans clustered about Jim Larkin, who was then in the country and making a name for himself as a roaring agitator. Ben was one of his devotees. Jim awed these young men with his large, lumbering body, his gruff voice, his self-adulation as a supreme revolutionist, an ascetic, a prophet, a seer. The prophet and ascetic stance was quite silly, since it was common knowledge that he was infatuated with a stage-struck daughter

Jim Larkin

of the bourgeoisie who had a finishing school education and a bohemian apartment on Patchin Place. Larkin's young followers seemed to take him uncritically and defend him against all attackers. Yes, Jim Larkin was a revolutionary hero among these young bohemians, but he could be insulting and offensive to Socialists and radicals with whom he did not agree. He would quarrel and brawl at meetings. For his satellites he could do no wrong.

I left New York in May [1917] and returned to Greenwich. I did not want to spend a summer in the city that held me so little. I now knew that I always could do something with my stenography. I also thought of the possibility of combining a bookshop with public stenographic work. The plan began to become a reality when a remodeled hotel on the Boston Post Road offered a modest shop adjoining at a low rent. I borrowed $200 and went into business. I worked endless hours to decorate the place; the front would be the bookshop and a small rear room was my stenography office. What little clientele I had came from the hotel, the Pickwick Arms, and some manuscript work. My

earnings were small and the book sales yielded little profit, but the overhead was low and so was my house rent. I lived in an apartment that had once been the chauffeur's quarters on a 14-acre estate with a palatial home. The gardener's cottage was opposite mine. It was the gardener, a Socialist and a friend, who told me of the apartment. The rent was $12 a month, and it was a lovely spot, but it was three miles from my business. I walked the distance twice a day.

The summer was a hard one, financially and emotionally. Ben was still seeking the chimerical theater job. In the meantime, he made an unsuccessful effort to produce a play in nearby Stamford and gave some readings which drew very few, but he spent most of his time in New York. When school vacations started he brought his three girls to stay with me for the summer.

In the fall two of my friends who were trainees at the Edgewood

School established on Marietta Johnson's Organic Education theory got Mrs. Johnson interested in the girls. Edgewood was an expensive school, but Fairhope, Alabama, where Mrs. Johnson had founded the original school, offered cheap living. Mrs. Johnson got some wealthy women interested in the Légère children, who could not be supported by either the father or the mother. She raised $1,500 for a year's maintenance in Fairhope and took the children down there. The girls were five, seven, and nine when they left in 1917. From then on, they were Mrs. Johnson's responsibility. Ben did nothing, or next to nothing, for them. They grew up at Fairhope. Years later the two younger girls joined their mother, who worked in Washington, D.C. The older one was married at eighteen to a Fairhope boy.

My business venture was unsuccessful. Once again, I took a job in New York. The Hebrew Sheltering and Immigrant Aid Society (HIAS) was making a survey of its work, and I got on the staff. I closed the Greenwich place and went to live with my sister, who then had an apartment in Greenwich Village.

The country was at war. The November revolution in Russia and the ascension of the Bolsheviks brought confusion and dissention among Socialists and other radicals. Persecution of war dissenters was rampant; Socialists, pacifists, IWWs were jailed by the hundreds. The patrioteers and the profiteers were in command. Americans were giving up their sons, husbands, and sweethearts, hypnotized by the propagandistic slogan that it was a "war to make the world safe for democracy." Woodrow Wilson's intellectualism was to most liberals a guarantee of integrity, and they suspended judgment. With them went many a Socialist intellectual: the Spargos and the Stokes and the Wallings and others. One saw them in their officers' uniforms, heard them and read

them in their justification of the "allies' cause"; I saw with bitterness the destruction of the international socialist movement.

There were shortages of food, of fuel, and for the poor, rationing. But the rich grew richer—investments were paying handsomely. In their silk shirts and silk stockings, they sneered at the workers. "War is the health of the state," wrote Randolph Bourne in his denunciation of war. The state was healthy and prospered while millions died.

With the establishment of the Soviets most of the radical movement in the United States threw its support to the New Russia. Everywhere the urge and excitement of giving aid to a people that had thrown off centuries of despotism was moving individuals and groups to speak and work and give financial and moral aid to the

Russian people. Unions and fraternal organizations, particularly those with a social background, opened their treasuries, collected funds, espoused in every way the new Socialist land. A decade later, disillusionment overtook many of them. Two decades later most of them were stunned by the atrocities and purges. Not long after followed the Stalin-Hitler pact and more and more betrayals of the revolution and the building of a totalitarian state. But those were unanticipated changes, and even as they began to show their sinister meaning many gave them the benefit of the doubt. For a long time it seemed even to sober-minded radicals that the revolution could do no wrong.

JOE ETTOR'S WIFE, IVA SCHUSTER, WELCOMED MATILDA back from Greenville. Although she seemed to dislike Ben, Iva offered friendship to Matilda, gave her temporary shelter, and was key to opening paths to better-paid employment. Ida urged Matilda to learn skills—typing and shorthand—that supported my grandmother for the rest of her life.

Few secretaries use shorthand now, but before the electronic era it was essential for taking accurate dictation, and practitioners were called stenographers. The only people I can think of who use shorthand today are journalists. It is surprising that Matilda learned the skill so rapidly, in a matter of weeks. I remember her half-sheet, spiral-bound notebooks filled with characters I couldn't read. Was it Russian? No, shorthand, she explained, and showed me how to read and write a few characters. She used the Gregg method.

Iva invited her to stay in New York again after Vita was born. The friendship continued when Iva and Joe relocated to California, where Matilda and Vita had also moved. Joe Ettor abandoned organizing, grew grapes, and made wine in Southern California. Matilda reared her daughter and found employment as a social worker, using the skills she developed with Ida's encouragement. Vita remembered picking dandelions with Iva in Southern California; Iva believed that using the plant in salads and other dishes could prevent, or even cure, cancer.

When summer came, Matilda, longing to leave New York, took a low-paying job in Greenwich, Connecticut, and Ben pursued her there. Eventually she had to return to find work in New York—at a bank. Instead of $12 a week working on the ill-fated *Our Town*, she earned $125 a month at Guaranty Trust!

Finally, Matilda had found a well-paid job that, with her secretarial skills and the languages she commanded, might have launched her upon an upward economic trajectory. Instead, it seems she turned her back on the offered opportunity to return to Russia, retreating instead to Greenwich again for the following summer, using her savings from the bank job to establish herself. Like her mother, she tried her hand at business. This business, though, was a bookstore and a stenography service, not a candy store or a grocery.

With Matilda's obligation to care for Ben's three daughters that summer, it's no wonder that the bookstore and stenography business made little money. Concerned about finding a stable situation for the children, daughters of a feckless father and an overwhelmed mother, she appealed to her friends, teachers from the nearby Edgewood School, who took an interest in the future of these girls. While it may surprise some that she willingly nurtured these girls, Matilda's adherence to free love was augmented by her natural affection for children and her compassion for Ben's daughters. Her friends introduced Matilda to Marietta Johnson's principles of "organic education" and suggested the girls apply to Johnson's school in the South, which was more affordable than the school nearby in Massachusetts. Benita, Elaine, and Jane must have stayed at Johnson's school in Fairhope, Alabama, for nine years. The school is still in operation there. In Ben's papers, I found scores of letters to their father from the girls "at boarding school." Over the years most messages are pleas from the daughters for small amounts of money. One example says something like, "my puppy has worms. Can you send me $1.00 so I can buy medicine for him so they don't put him to sleep?" There are similar letters from his first and last wives filled with the minutiae of domestic financial matters, usually requesting urgent assistance from Ben ("The insurance payments are due," etc.). And from what I can tell, he was rarely able to help, pleading that he was short himself.

Among Ben's papers I found a series of exchanges between Matilda and Ben about a clock. Sometime in the 1930s Matilda agreed to a meeting between Vita and her father, so she began to communicate with Ben. A comrade had agreed to repair a clock for Matilda, and Ben somehow had been the intermediary for the arrangement. There are several terse postcards from my grandmother regarding other arrangements, as well, but also reminding him that she wanted her clock returned, repaired or not. His archive abounds with material like this.

Opposed to the United States entering World War I, Matilda briefly mentions how the decision rent the Socialist Party and, in her eyes, was a major factor in the dissolution of international Socialism. Her own brother Morris enlisted. Many Wobblies went to jail for opposing the war. Exceptions to Matilda's assertion that the Socialist intelligentsia joined liberals in supporting the war, two of the notable couples that she claims abandoned their Socialist principles in support of the war were not unified in their opinion. Rose Pastor Stokes, a

ANNA STRUNSKY WALLING

prominent Russian Jewish leftist, worked in a cigar factory for four-teen years. She met and married the wealthy Graham Phelps Stokes, a settlement house worker, who joined the war effort and became an officer in the U.S. military. Rose was outspokenly opposed to her husband's support for the war, which probably was a major factor in their divorce. Matilda's friend Anna Strunsky Walling also disagreed with her husband, William English Walling, who supported the war.

Husband and wife never reconciled their disagreement, and they too eventually divorced.

From her few comments about the Russian Revolution, it's hard to tell how it affected Matilda at the time. Her assessment of what followed is born of decades of reflection. A "sober-minded radical" like Matilda questioned the orthodoxy of the party lines. Especially relevant today is her quote from Randolph Bourne, "War is the health of the state," and her added observation that the state is healthy and prospers while millions die. Antiwar Socialists, fewer and fewer as the United States prepared to join the allies, believed that participating in military adventures supported capitalist interests at the expense of workers' lives. Soldiers were mere cannon fodder.

12   A NEW LIFE (VITA)

After my job with the HIAS I took one with the Joint Distribution Committee, organized to give aid to Jews in the war countries. With Julian Leavitt, I worked on a survey and report, which served as a guide to a delegation to those countries. When this was completed I was assigned to organize and direct a branch office for the JDC. It was fall of 1918. I had spent the spring and summer in the Greenwich apartment, commuting to New York. Ben, essentially living there with me, shifted between the theater agencies and the agitating Irish radicals, some of whom would spend occasional weekends with us in Greenwich. It was a cruelly unhappy summer.

Once again we parted. Ben got a part with a road company playing *The Bird of Paradise*, and he left abruptly. I let some friends have the Greenwich place for a couple of the fall months and went to live in New York. Soon I knew that I was pregnant.

The following months were among the happiest I had known. I shared an apartment with two young German women, Elsa Tenhardt and Erna Schneeweiss. The apartment was on the roof of an apartment house facing Central Park West, a very high-rent district. Our three rooms—one shaped like a submarine looking out on the park and the other two, the kitchen and another room behind it—were probably originally either storage rooms or perhaps used by a janitor or elevator man. Our rent was $55 a month. We rode up in the elegant elevator to the top floor and then walked up a short flight of steps to our roof. The roof was a delightful veranda, with a view of New York which we enjoyed from our deck chairs. It was a rare boon for me. I rode on the bus down to Washington Square and walked a short distance to my office. Washington Square was the beginning of the line, so I always had a seat on the way home, and on pleasant days I sat outside on the top deck of the bus.

We lived frugally, yet quite graciously, doing our own cooking and laundry as well as some of our sewing. The girls were interesting and took such interest in me and the coming baby. Elsa, who was a student at Columbia earning her way by translations and library work, would occasionally bring Hindu and German students to the apartment. Erna was a chemistry technician, petite and gentle, as Elsa was inclined to be critical and harsh. Erna was in love with a biologist who was employed in the same laboratory. He was also a visitor to the apartment, and he appeared to be in love with her. There was music and talk, contention and arguments about the war.

I left New York on the last day of May 1919. I went by boat to Boston (through the Metropolitan Canal, no longer in service), then by train to New Bedford and from there by boat to Nantucket, 30 miles from the mainland. Phyllis and Jay Cisco met me at the landing in their car, one of only three on the island at the time. Thus, three of the loveliest months of my life began.

Nantucket has a stern charm. Its skies are mostly gray, its houses prim, its fences mended, its hollyhocks erect, its natives sedate and standoffish. One is always an off-islander, unless descended from the old settlers. Summer residents are just so many aliens who invade the island for three months and are well rid of. The natives are proud of their history—always the great whaling days, never the slave trade or Indian extermination. The Macys, the Starbucks, the Folgers, the Coffins, these remain the proud names on the island; the days of whaling glory have long since departed and now their livelihood depends mostly on summer visitors.

The two months before the baby came were long, and then there were two tranquil, sleepy, lazy days in the hospital before my daughter, Vita, was born.

In July 1919, at the time Vita was born, there was a little ten-bed cottage hospital on the island which was mainly used for summer visitors' confinement cases. Native islanders still had their babies at home. My doctor who had practiced on the island for 25 years had delivered over 1,500 babies, all at home. My baby was one of three born in the hospital during the three weeks I was there. Two weeks was a normal stay for a confinement case, but I stayed an extra week because my cabin had been painted and the paint wouldn't dry. Once the 16-hour labor was over, the three weeks in the hospital were altogether delightful. My room looked out on a garden. Since there were still chilly evenings even in July and August, I was happy to have a little fireplace in the room.

There is no joy comparable to that of seeing one's cherished infant for the first time. Still only half conscious when the nurse brought her to me, I was deliriously happy with my baby. No thought disturbed me: the past receded, the future I would not think about. Only the present mattered. The present held everything.

I returned from the hospital to my one-room cabin. It was sparsely furnished with only the bare necessities: a cot for me, the baby's basket, a small table, one chair, a kerosene stove, an oil lamp. The floor was bare, the walls were a warm knotty pine, and I had made yellow curtains for the windows. Water I carried from the Ciscos' house, then heated it on the stove and washed the baby's things in a small galvanized tub. They dried on a line hung between the house and a post in the salty, windy air.

Now it was mid-August, and in three weeks I would be leaving. I

had only a few dollars left of the $150 I had brought with me. What was I going to do for a living? I planned to return to the Greenwich place. The rent had been paid for the last few months by some friends who had taken it for the summer. It would be mine again in September.

"IT WAS A CRUELLY UNHAPPY SUMMER," MATILDA laments. No doubt Ben's solipsism, his comings and goings, and her irritation with visits from the Irish nationalists to whom Ben was so attracted contributed to her unhappiness. His failure to contribute to their expenses was no doubt galling. In some of the half-finished stories found in the archives, there is a parasitic male character connected to a woman who provides meals, a bed, and car fare. He never reciprocates.

Ben joined a stock company in a traveling production of *The Bird of Paradise*, a popular Broadway play intended to convey a serious message expressing sympathy for the plight of native Hawaiians. Cheesy music and spectacle made it financially successful for years to follow. Its racialized tropes of the "noble savage" and the dark, doomed beauty resonated with audiences fascinated by tourism, exotic locales, and notions of eugenics. In spite of the unhappiness of that summer in Greenwich, there were obviously moments of intimacy between Ben and Matilda, since she tells us, "Soon I knew that I was pregnant."

In the fall she returned to work in New York City with the American Jewish Joint Distribution Committee and had a few months of warmth, support, and conviviality living with German roommates on the Upper West Side. This is a joyous entry in the memoir. She obviously had a wonderful pregnancy—oblivious, or at least unconcerned, about the risks she knew she was taking physically and socially. She doesn't speculate on her German roommates' experience in the United States during a time when America was preparing to go to war, and when nativism flourished, even on the left. Germany and the

Kaiser were reviled, and America's stance toward Germany split the Socialists. William English Walling reveals his hatred of Germany in his writing from this period, and other prominent Socialists support-ed America's entry into the war—G. P. Stokes, Upton Sinclair, many in the Socialist Party. Debs of course adhered to his principles. The anti-German feelings were high. All Matilda tells us is that there were arguments about the war. The arguments, according to what I have read, were ferocious and ended decades-long friendships and at least a few marriages.

I remember her saying that she "showed" very little during her pregnancy—her condition was not obvious—and possibly in the cir-cles she traveled, few noticed or cared.

I am grateful for her vivid evocation of Nantucket, and the hap-piness she describes during the months she spent there is rhapsodic. She barely mentions the pain of childbirth, and her three weeks' hos-pital confinement is described as pleasant, which contrasts with my own experience and that of most mothers I know.

Matilda embraced motherhood with lyricism and even more pas-sion than she did the IWW and with no ambivalence, in contrast to the decades-long romantic involvement with Ben. Her joy is pure, nothing like the grinding effort she describes in her work as an orga-nizer.

She was fortunate to have relationships with a number of well-connected Socialists during this period of her life and the years that followed. Her friends on Nantucket, Jay and Phyllis Cisco, must have been among these left-leaning, artistic connections. More bohemian than politically radical, the Ciscos were rich Socialists and arts lovers. Jay Cisco, from a family of wealth, Harvard graduate, and Wall Street lawyer, inherited the family property on Nantucket. Their home at this time was on the north shore of the island, but today, on the south shore, Cisco Beach is named for these "summer people." Jay's father is said to have taken long, reflective walks on that beach, where he solved legal and financial problems. Matilda had saved some money, but the Ciscos' interest and support surely made the idyll of Vita's birth possible.

Although Matilda might chafe at the suggestion, the birth of her daughter must have changed her self-identity as agitator. Her need to support her child and desire for a congenial social milieu led her toward associations with notable bohemians and some of the important progressive intellectuals of her time, and so she began to explore the role of a wage-earning, single mother of the left.

13   BEN RETURNS

It was a beautiful autumn. I settled back in the Greenwich apartment. The estate remained unsold, and there were acres of beautiful trees massed in browns and yellows along with flaming sumac and a late-flowering vine here and there. My good Socialist comrade was still in his gardener's cottage with his wife and two girls. I felt at home and happy, so happy with my baby! But the next six months were trying months financially. Although my living expenses were small, I had no income of any kind and I had to borrow. My brother David and my sister, Minnie, helped. They came often on weekends. My old friends Corinne and Dorothy visited me and brought Helen Boyd, who later came to live with me in New York. I was determined to have a year, Vita's first year, away from jobs, away from the strains and tensions of a city. I wanted tranquility and the pleasure of motherhood.

One night in November I was awakened by a door opening. It had been raining and blustery, and I thought the wind had blown it open. I got up to close it, without turning on the light. But it had already closed, and wet and trembling Ben stood beside it. My immediate impulse was to order him to leave, but I couldn't speak. He held out his arms. I turned the light on, and seeing the crib he walked over to it. Bending down over it he sobbed out, "I didn't know . . . You never let me know . . . I can't bear to leave you."

We talked and talked through the night. What had be been doing? He told me about his three months on the road with a stock company and an affair with an actress in the show, the same bohemian over whom Jim Larkin lost his head. He had been unable to get another job in the theater, but he was still trying to make a place for himself in the labor movement. He had been trying to promote the One Big Union in Lawrence where there had been a sort of revival of organization. The girls? They were well and being cared for at the Fairhope School. It was the same old pattern that I knew so well, and yet I found myself drawn to this man who had given me no happiness in the past and who would, I knew, bring torment into my life again. I knew, I knew, and yet he was irresistible and I was in his arms again.

Winter set in, lovely and cold. Snow fell, the country was white, the trees sparkled, icicles hung from the roof and at my windows. Across the road the Edgewood School grounds were colorful with the reds and greens and blues of the children's snow suits and caps, and the air rang with their shouts at play. Through the bare branches of the trees I watched them throwing snowballs and playing on their sleds. The heating in the apartment was inadequate, the only source being a portable heater which I carried from the small combination living room-kitchen to the bedroom and back again. I had lived there only during the summer and fall until this year. I now discovered that the place was not equipped for winter living, but I was determined to stay on; I did not know where else to go with the baby.

My friend Anna Walling who visited me occasionally was worried. She, with her husband, William English Walling, and their four children, lived not far from us. The daughter of a comfortably situated family, married to Walling who was rich, Anna had never known hardship. Walling was a well-known Socialist and a writer of Socialist books. At the time I had the bookshop in Greenwich and was doing stenography, I had done some work for him. Naturally irascible, the war aggravated his relationship with his wife, who strongly disagreed with his position. Anna remained the internationalist while Walling,

along with other Socialist intellectuals, became militantly prowar. Their marriage weathered the disagreement, however, and they remained together.

Anna was a charming, warm-hearted, sensitive person, who always seemed uncomfortable in the pretentious setting of her big house and servants and in the company of the conventional matrons whose children were at the Edgewood School with her own.

She happened to visit one day when I was carrying water from the gardener's cottage to my apartment. There had been a severe cold spell in January when the water main connecting my supply had frozen for an eighth of a mile down the line. Water pipes were frozen all around, the cost of repair was high, and plumbers hard to get. Anna, horrified by the situation, would not leave until I agreed to go home with her and stay until water was available.

We stayed at the Walling home three weeks. Except for the first week when I came down with an attack of tonsillitis, it was a pleasant stay. Walling was in his study most of the time writing, and Anna went to New York to the theater or to visit her family once or twice a week. Then I would have dinner with the children alone and read to them before bedtime. Sometimes they would come up to our room to see the baby, whom they looked upon as a beautiful, big doll—that was a special treat.

When I went back to the apartment again, it was only to pack up for another journey. For while I was at the Wallings, a plan developed to go to New Hampshire. Mary Chase, a young trainee at the Edgewood School, sometimes came to visit with my friends Corinne and Dorothy Decker, who were teachers at the school. Mary's home was in New Hampshire, and she suggested that I go up to stay with her mother who had a big house and wanted some company through the winter. Mary wrote her mother about me, and soon I had an invitation from Mrs. Chase asking me and my six-month-old baby, Vita, to stay with her.

Why did Ben come along? Why did I allow it? Practically on the eve of my departure he arrived from New York, contrite, pleading, begging forgiveness. Having unburdened himself of his feelings of guilt, he begged permission to go with us to New Hampshire, and I let him come.

It was a singular journey. From the nearest direct train station, Bellows Falls, Vermont, we rode the ten miles to E. Alstead, New Hampshire, in a smoky little train; the next four miles to Mill Hollow and the Chase home we traveled by sleigh. It was an unforgettably beautiful ride. The snow-packed road ran through majestic pine woods as the sleigh runners rent the deep silence like cutting silk. We were silent, too. The baby slept. I was lost in this beautiful, somber, silent world.

Margaret Chase and Hartley Dennett, her companion, received us warmly. We sat before the fire and talked until quite late. Ben stayed until midafternoon the next day, and left reluctantly. He would have stayed on. He had no qualms about staying on—another day and then another. But this was not my own home, and I insisted that he must not stay any longer. He was gloomy and resentful. How long would I stay, he importuned. As long as I could, I replied. He did not ask how I was going to meet expenses. He no doubt thought that I would accept free room and board, as he had done so often in his life.

My arrangement with Margaret was to pay a dollar a day and to help with housekeeping. The latter was easy. While the Brick House, as they called their home, was a large two-story seven-room house, Margaret and Hartley lived very simply. The furnishings consisted of beautiful old colonial pieces. The spacious rooms were uncluttered, and the fireplace was ample. There was almost a continuous fire, although the lower floors had forced heat. One could indulge in wood burning in New Hampshire with well-seasoned wood at only eight dollars a cord.

After many evenings' conversation before the fire I came to know my hosts' story, while they learned of my life. Margaret Chase was about fifty when I came to the Brick House, and Hartley Dennett was somewhat younger. They had come to Mill Hollow a dozen years earlier, he a divorced man and she separated, but not divorced. Both of them left Boston after a stormy divorce suit in which Hartley's wife, Mary Ware Dennett, named Margaret as the correspondent. Both

families were prominent in professional circles, Hartley as a success-ful architect, and Margaret's husband as a physician. Mary Ware Dennett and Margaret were both active in the suffrage movement, and Mrs. Dennett was known as an advocate of birth control.

The families were close friends and, with their children, spent their summers together in the country. It was during these vacations that a warm friendship developed between Margaret and Hartley. Between vacations there was correspondence. It had been all platon-ic, Margaret insisted, involving discussions of ethics, esthetics, edu-cation, and philosophy. Both of them were influenced by Emerson. But platonic or not, Mary Dennett objected to their friendship and sued for divorce. The ensuing publicity all but crushed Hartley, and though it was a shock to Margaret, it was more bearable for her. She separated from Dr. Chase, a Quaker, who would have no divorce, but the children went with her. Mary Dennett was granted full custody of their two boys. Apparently Hartley could not bear up under the situation, he could not marry Margaret, but they would remain friends and companions. They made the difficult decision to go away together (I always felt it was Margaret's decision), to leave Boston and their friends. Hartley abandoned his profession, and they isolated themselves in rural New Hampshire.

Whatever mental anguish they may have suffered was not aggravated by material want. Hartley had an independent income, and Margaret and the children were well provided for by Dr. Chase, who remained a warm friend. He visited once during my stay, and I found him a gentle, self-effacing person, the opposite of self-assertive, harsh Margaret. Hartley, too, was mild-mannered, retiring, but friendly. Obviously, Margaret dominated both men. She carried an air of martyrdom: the world misunderstood her pure intentions, her high-mindedness, and the price she paid for her integrity.

I naturally assumed that Margaret and Hartley, having gone the unconventional way, were living as man and wife without benefit of clergy. Margaret certainly showed her strength as an emancipated woman, and I admired her for it, being myself an emancipated woman. She in turn respected my radicalism, my former activity in the labor movement, my fulfilled desire to have and to rear a child without dependence on the father. Then one evening during dinner I praised Mary Ware Dennett's pamphlet on birth control. I described my acquaintance with Margaret Sanger and a bit of propaganda on birth control in which I had engaged. My hostess pursed her lips, and an indignant look hardened her face. She was far from good-looking, and now the bitter twist of the mouth, the squared shoulders, the hard look made her much less so. The sudden silence made me uncomfortable. Then Margaret, in a superior tone, said icily, "The kind of birth control I believe in is self-control." Her declaration was so final and so self-righteous that I was glad to drop the subject. We never referred to it again.

Then a few days later I was taking a walk with a friend of Margaret's on a visit from Boston. They had long known each other, and she held our hostess in great esteem. She had stood by her in the trying days of the divorce, and she now spoke with great emotion about the injustice and pain that had been inflicted on Margaret by Mary Dennett's erroneous understanding of her. Margaret's decision to leave the old life and isolate herself with Hartley was not only to get away from the censure and ostracism, but to prove to the world that one could have companionship and even love for a man—even live together, share the same bedroom—without sexual intercourse. Self-control, Margaret's armor, was forever kept shining.

The woman must have sensed my astonishment, but misinterpreting it she belabored the subject by emphasizing how wrong people were who thought that Margaret and Hartley lived as man and wife. In truth, I did not understand. Why? Why suffer the propinquity? Why subject a man and a woman for years to an unnatural relationship? That was what Margaret wanted. That was the condition she insisted upon as they left their old world. The friend was emphatic in letting me know, in case I too misunderstood the facts in the case.

Margaret ran the affairs of Brick House like a general with Hartley a willing subaltern. He looked much older than his years, soft-spoken, slow-moving, and likable. They both seemed to love the country and spent their time collecting antiques, buying land, old houses, and old mills. Life was completely uneventful month in, month out. The school holidays brought Margaret's two children home, Mary about 20 and Herman, 18. Except for the one visit from Dr. Chase and Margaret's friend, I remember no other visitors during my three-month stay at Brick House, nor in the months I lived near it.

The attitude of the natives in this rural New England village amazed me. They regarded the Chase-Dennett arrangement with a perplexed tolerance—this man and woman living together, but going

under their own names. Were they married, or not? What about the former husband visiting? They did not attend any church, had little relation with the natives, although they were always ready to help in any emergency. They bought milk and wood from the local people, and some groceries from the store four miles from Mill Hollow in the larger village of E. Alstead. They made their own maple sugar in the sugar house in the woods about a half mile from the house. I helped with the sugar making, but they never had any paid help either there or in the home.

Both of them were abstemious and thrifty to an extreme. Margaret bought the discarded but very excellent woolen cloth, used on the roller in making paper, from the nearby mill and made it into blankets and coats for herself and Mary. There were always quantities of root vegetables in the cellar, pickles, preserves, cured meats, cheeses. When I moved to my own house in the spring they sold me some potatoes and turnips.

I enjoyed my days at the Brick House. The weather was mostly at zero and below. The snow was deep and hard, and we used snowshoes to get about. I was well and continued to nurse Vita, now seven months old, and soon began to wean her on whole cow's milk. I read; there was some music on phonograph records; there were the evenings before the fire, when Margaret sometimes read to us, usually essays of the transcendentalists. It was at such hours that Hartley seemed the tired old man. I felt here that Margaret's reading had no substance for him; that it was a kind of narcotic that would often put him to sleep. Margaret would read on, unrelaxed, annoyed by Hartley's inattention. We retired early.

Spring comes slowly in New Hampshire. It wasn't until early in May that I moved into my own place. This was the lower part of an old house built sometime around the Revolutionary War. It had been unoccupied for many years, but was solid enough. Margaret and Hartley had acquired it along with other pieces of property in the neighborhood. It stood on the edge of a small lake. A much-neglected garden led down to it. It was about a third of a mile across and later I would swim the distance. A nice accomplishment for me, who was a poor swimmer.

The upper part of the house was later occupied by another family, but my part consisted of a large living room, a bedroom, and a spacious kitchen. I pulled out the bricks which had closed off the fireplace and the side oven and built a fire on a hearth four feet wide. Swallows who had been nesting in the chimney for many of their generations were smoked out, but they kept coming back when there was

no fire. Then one day some came down the chimney into the living room. In great confusion they flew about the room trying to get out, beating against walls and windows. Most of them got out as I threw open doors and windows. But there were some casualties.

I gathered a few pieces of furniture from Margaret's attics including an old cradle for Vita and a few dishes, scrubbed the wide and worn planks of the floors, put some short yellow curtains on the small-paned windows, and placed some old kerosene lamps with bright chimneys in dark corners. There was always a pile of cut wood for the fireplace and the kitchen stove. There was a clean stone cellar for the vegetables and dairy foods. Groceries from the store at E. Alstead were brought up in an old Ford twice a week in the summer only. I bought milk every day from the nearest farm a half-mile away. And in midsummer I gathered a nice crop of vegetables from my own garden.

It was a lovely summer and a lovely fall. I didn't want to think of the future. The days went by blissfully. My baby played in the pen on the lawn under an old elm, the lake at the back door and the old rowboat nearby. The few good friends that came and went during the summer were ample company: Corinne, Dorothy, my brother David, my sister. Old Professor Simon Patterson spent his summers at Mill Hollow living in a little shack in the pines. Past seventy, he was hardy and spirited. Every day, when the weather was good and he wasn't writing, he would put in some hours mending the road. He spent many an evening at my fireside talking economics and discussing current events. He was a liberal, concerned with postwar repressions: the imprisonment of Eugene Debs, the radicals, pacifists, and the IWWs. Sometimes we were joined by Mrs. Rawson, who occupied the second story of the house, and sometimes Margaret would come by or Mr. Smith, a summer visitor. But on the whole I saw few people during that summer.

Ben came for a brief visit and brought Jane, one of his children. Jane was ten, a delicate and moody child. She stayed several weeks. Ben was engaged in some organizing work in Lawrence, Massachusetts. He was now in disrepute with the IWW and was promoting his own brand of One Big Union. It was not until years later that I learned of the dissension he sowed and his egotistical assumption of authority, his "bad actor" performance.

We had not seen each other in six months. But the reunion was not a happy one. It was July, and Vita was now a year old. Soon I would

have to move on: to a city, a job, a home for me and my baby. I had no prospects. I lived on about $30 a month, and all of it was borrowed. Ben offered no help, as usual, and I did not expect it. I considered the possibility of remaining here through the winter, perhaps even another year.

Margaret urged me to remain. If I insisted on setting out in search of a job, she offered to take Vita. As she put it, "I'll take her until she is one or twenty-one."

"Now, Margaret," I replied, "Why do you think I had her?" and we both laughed. The question never came up again, but she was sincerely concerned, showed her dislike of Ben, and was critical of his lack of responsibility.

"How can he bring Jane for you to care for and never offer a grain of help?"

Well, that was an old story, and I expected no help. When I decided to have a child, I was fully aware that it would be my sole responsibility. Neither for the first, nor the second, nor the third, nor the fourth wife, nor for any of their children did Ben ever provide, and his legal obligations to me and Vita were even smaller.

Then I got a letter in September from my closest friend, Marie Hourwich (Kravitz), then living in Washington. What were my plans? Would I consider coming to Washington? Her daughter, Helen, was nearly three, and Marie was considering taking a job. She had been with the Children's Bureau before Helen was born. Her husband, Aaron, was with the Federal Trade Commission. She had a tentative plan, if I would consider coming. Should she get a job before me, I would take on the care of Helen. If I were to get one first, she would take on the care of Vita. We could share the expense of a housekeeper and generally work out cooperative arrangements.

I jumped at the proposal. Here was a light in a bleak situation. At the end of September I left Mill Hollow and the happiest months of my life. How I longed to stay! The memories of those months blend with those of Nantucket, and not even the intervening unhappy days with Ben ever could make that first year less joyous.

Bellows Falls, Vermont, is only about 14 miles from East Alstead and reached by bus to make train connections. I should have gone directly to Boston and on to Washington. But once again I succumbed to entreaties from Ben to stop off at Lawrence. We spent a week in a horrible rooming house and in a horrible mood. Ben was squabbling with union members, had made a number of enemies, and was on the way out. Fred Beal (who became a Communist and wrote a book recounting his experiences) years later told me of the struggle with Ben and his brand of OBU [One Big Union.]

"He never was really an organizer; he was always the actor. I would hear him rehearsing a speech and watching himself in the mirror. He would never appear on the platform until the chairman made an introductory and laudatory speech about him. Then he would step out to receive the applause. An actor, always an actor. He had no place in the labor movement."

Amusingly, Beal always confused me with Barbara, Ben's lover after me. He thought he had met me in Lawrence. He probably did, but he also may have met Barbara; he did not remember. Anyway, he had us mixed up and never did straighten the matter out and was still puzzled when I saw him in Los Angeles in 1952.

I did not see Ben's performance as organizer, since the meetings were always in the evening and I could not leave Vita. I did see the moodiness and the discontent, and I heard the carping criticism. It was too much. Our feelings were already strained to the breaking point. I left Lawrence with a sense of relief and a determination to end our relationship. I still had much to learn.

"HE WAS IRRESISTIBLE AND I WAS IN HIS ARMS AGAIN."

It is difficult to understand Matilda's decades-long involvement with Ben. Little given to introspection or self-criticism, she rarely examines her psychological state. Though Matilda and Ben were initially united by politics and love of literature, one can only guess that much of their attachment was erotic. Although she prided herself on self-sufficiency and discipline, she managed to afford a year without earned income, perhaps using some of the same strategies Ben employed to avoid labor that was boring and distasteful—borrowing money and accepting gifts.

Matilda was aware of Ben's affair while he was on tour with one of the actresses in the cast, the "stage-struck daughter of the bourgeoisie who had a finishing school education and a bohemian apartment on Patchin Place," who had been Jim Larkin's lover. Embracing the free love ideal, she didn't express jealousy, asserting that she was free to do the same, although she rarely, perhaps never, did.

It's odd that Matilda refers to Anna Walling only by her married name, as she was better known as the writer and outspoken Socialist Anna Strunsky. She was, like Matilda, a Russian Jewish immigrant, although from a middle-class family. Strunsky grew up in San Francisco, attended Stanford, and was featured as the "Girl Socialist" in a *San Francisco Examiner* article (October 3, 1897) about her lecture on the ethics of Socialism. She was member of a bohemian circle of artists and writers known as the "Crowd." It was in this milieu that she became a close friend of Jack London, with whom she wrote an epistolary novel, *The Kempton-Wace Letters*, London's only known collaboration. Years later, when Matilda and I were living in Berkeley, she mentioned that she had recently seen her friend Joan London. Joan was Jack's daughter (like the father who abandoned her, a Socialist) and part of Matilda's social network.

Anna's husband, William English Walling, known as English, was the aristocratic son of a wealthy and prestigious Kentucky family. Educated at the University of Chicago, Walling wrote about the conditions of the poor and became a settlement house worker in Chicago. He and Strunsky, having met in settlement house work in the mid-1900s and as supporters of the 1905 Russian Revolution, fell in love in St. Petersburg, journalists covering the revolution's aftermath.

Matilda barely mentions working for Walling, and he doesn't much interest her, but he was a prolific writer and highly regarded as a thinker among progressives. Though he was from a family of slave owners, he was an advocate for civil rights and a founder of the National Association for the Advancement of Colored People. A friend of W. E. B. Du Bois, he had public disagreements with Booker T. Washington's conservatism and his belief that Negros must "earn" their civil rights.

The Walling marriage was the subject of scandal, not for their different religious backgrounds, but because of a very public lawsuit for breach of promise brought by Anna Berthe Grunspan, a Russian

Jewish woman whom Walling met in Paris, where they had a brief affair. She was only sixteen at the time. Booker T. Washington found the notoriety of the lawsuit disgraceful and called for cutting all organizational ties to Walling. Strunsky supported her husband and attended the trial.

Matilda says that the Walling marriage weathered their disagreement about the war, but in fact, they ultimately divorced. Walling became a jingoistic supporter of Woodrow Wilson, writing articles with headlines such as "Socialism: The Kaiser Party."

Introduced by friends of friends, Matilda accepted an offer of lodging in rural New Hampshire with Margaret Chase and her companion, Hartley Dennett, in the winter of 1920. The Dennetts and the Chases were not Socialists but advocates of Henry George's single-tax theory, although they were attracted to some principles of Socialism. Romantics interested in philosophy and literature, they were New England intellectuals, artistic and spiritual, not members of any organized religion. Hartley Dennett was a prominent architect, and his former wife, Mary Dennett, whose advocacy work Matilda admired, was not only an antiwar activist, a suffragist, and a promoter of birth control, but also an artist and designer, an adherent of the Arts and Crafts Movement. She had revived the lost art of guadamaçiles, a leather craft that originated in North Africa, flourished during the Caliphate of Córdoba in Spain beginning in the Middle Ages, and was practiced up to the eighteenth century. Prior to her years as an activist, she was head of the Department of Decoration and Design at the Drexel Institute of Art in Philadelphia, where she taught from 1894 to 1897.

When Mary Ware Dennett founded the National Birth Control League in 1915, she invited Margaret Sanger to sit on the board, but Sanger refused. Dennett's pamphlet "The Sex Side of Life: An Explanation for Young People," written for her sons at about the same time as the NBCL was formed, had been widely distributed through the YMCA, churches, and other organizations for youth since its first publication in 1918. More than a decade later, in 1929, Dennett was sued in federal court for distributing illegal material through the U.S. mail, a violation of the Comstock Act. Matilda probably had more admiration for Mary Ware Dennett's activism than for Margaret and Hartley's aestheticism rooted in New England Puritanism. While Margaret did not admit to participating in the free love idea, she certainly accepted Matilda and her baby. Margaret and Dr. Heman Lincoln Chase did eventually divorce, notwithstanding his Quakerism, and their children spent most of their lives in East Alstead, with Margaret and Hartley, where they remained into old age.

Matilda's contentment in Mill Hollow had more to do with her love of nature and the quiet, simple life she led there than with her affection for her hosts. The elderly professor she mentions was not "Patterson," but Dr. Simon Patten, an influential professor of economics at the Wharton School of Business at the University of Pennsylvania. He believed in an "economy of abundance" and that social and technological progress would end problems of scarcity. His opposition to World War I and his support of his colleague Scott Nearing led to his forced retirement at age sixty-five. Regarded as eccentric, but respected, he visited Mill Hollow every summer for many years, living during the summers in a small cabin in the woods, affecting the appearance of a wanderer, unshaven and long-haired, and well known for his enthusiasm for road repair.

I have not found any information about exactly what Ben was guilty of as an organizer in Lawrence, or about "his brand" of One Big Union. He must have begun his affair with Barbara Feningston by this time, because Matilda, who also visited Ben in Lawrence, believes that Fred Beal may have met Barbara there. Perhaps Ben's philandering was one cause of the misery she describes. If so, she is silent about it, adhering to the free love ideal. Ben brought one of his daughters to be looked after by Matilda for the summer again. Matilda seems to have had special sympathy for Jane and willingly included her in her family. Once again she is determined to end the relationship, but does not yet break it off.

14   WASHINGTON

Marie received me warmly. But I found that she wasn't too eager to take a job. Aaron was earning a fair salary, and there was no pressing need for her to do so. For me it was an immediate and pressing necessity. In a day or two I was in Washington and registered with an employment agency. My knowledge of shorthand and typing put me in the secretarial classification. At the end of my interview with the director of the agency—Scientific Placement Bureau, it was called—she asked me if, for the time being, I would take a half-day job there. She wanted someone to assist her in taking applications, keeping records, etc. The hours were 9 a.m. to 1 p.m., five days a week, for $75 a month. Later there might be a full-time job. Anyway, I was free to accept a more desirable job whenever one was offered. I already knew that jobs outside of government work were hard to get, but $75 a month would not be half enough to support us. I would be in a position to watch for other, better jobs, so I took the job, hoping for better.

I made arrangements for Vita to be cared for by Marie's landlady, Mrs. Stilson, who, with her husband and two sons, about 10 and 12, occupied the rear part of the three-family house where the Kravitzes had the lower half. She was eager to take Vita, an adorable, happy baby of 14 months, just taking her first steps. With Marie near to

221

keep an eye on things, I felt quite secure. But there was no need for any worry. Mrs. Stilson turned out to be a fine foster-mother. She loved the baby, and the entire family was devoted to her. The two boys, Walter and Carl, played with her, and Carl, particularly, loved to take her out in her go-cart.

I went to live with friends of the Kravitzes, Max and Sonia Zasuly. They had a large apartment, and I had a small room and breakfast and dinner with them during the week days. My weekends I spent with Vita in Takoma Park. The Zasulys were interesting people. Max worked for the Bureau of Standards. He was a romantic, excitable, and fond of conversation and music. And so was Sonia, who also was a prodigious reader of fiction and biography. Their ten-year-old son, Dick, was a pleasant and quiet child who suffered from a mild form of asthma, naturally causing the parents great concern. When I saw him some years later he seemed to have largely overcome the condition.

Then there was Isidore Lattman, who also had a room and board with the family. He was a pharmacist and was studying medicine. Isidore was short, swarthy, near-sighted. He was a great music lover. He claimed friendship with young musicians of the day, [Jascha] Heifetz, [Efrem] Zimbalist, who were said to have come from the same part of the Ukraine as he, and others. He was also a braggart. But still very likeable. And he was in love with Sonia. She was ten or more years older than Isidore. But they seemed to have much in common, especially music. Although neither of them played any instrument, they moved in a musical circle and were devoted supporters of chamber music concerts.

My living costs at the Zasulys were low, the environment pleasant. They had many friends; there were musical evenings and discussions of current events, books, etc. Mrs. Stilson charged only $40 a month for Vita's care. But the $75 a month was not enough. Fortunately, I soon had another job.

The SPB prided itself on placing only select and superior office workers. The owner and manager was a capable and shrewd woman who developed a source of revenue quite beside employment fees. Washington's tens of thousands of women workers in government offices had little opportunity to escape into other fields. Nor did most of them want to. But there were still a great many who tried to break out of the monotony and the poor rewards, for all the job security. For such seekers there were anglers that promised happier hunting grounds. There were the modern soothsayers who traded in "mind science"—various numerologists, phrenologists, psychics, spiritualists, mystics literate and illiterate—parasites who lived off the desire of thousands of frustrated government workers. Among these was Mrs. X of the SPB. The business on the side was Scientific Counsel. The employment placement was legitimate enough; the regular fees prescribed. The snare was for some who had ambition to break with their commonplace jobs and sought to rise. Here Mrs. X would advise a consultation to determine the aptitudes and possibilities of the applicant. She would charge ten dollars for a session after which a drawn chart resembling a phrenologist's would be issued to the consultee. Presumably, this would indicate the best features of the ambitious one that needed only to be worked on to produce success. The burden of proof was on the individual. Ah well, these counselors were not too far from the latter day "peace-of-mind positive-thinking" fraternity. They were less educated and less paid, less advertised and on the whole less harmful.

A month after I came to the SPB a call came in from the Knights of Columbus Rehabilitation School for a secretary to the director, Dr. Frank O'Hara. The KC were running a number of these evening schools throughout the country, offering courses in English and commercial subjects to ex-servicemen and -women. We sent out two or three of the best-qualified secretaries, but they were not acceptable. Mrs. X was surprised and chagrined. What sort of genius did Dr. O'Hara want, anyway? We had none better. Could I try for the job? Well, yes, if I wanted to—but she didn't think it was what I would want. She hoped I would consider it carefully. She would like for me

to stay with the bureau—there may be a full-time job later. I reassured her. If I did get the job with the KC, I could still stay on, since the hours there were from 2 p.m. to 9 p.m. combining office and evening school hours. So I applied for the job.

Dr. O'Hara interviewed me in his office. He was a gracious, cultivated person, apparently broad-minded in his social attitude. I was naturally careful to put forth my most conventional references: the Guaranty Trust of New York, the *New York Tribune*, the Children's Bureau, the Joint Distribution Committee (my last job before Vita was born), and such others as would have no connection with union organization. Dr. O'Hara was an associate professor of economics at the Catholic University, and so he naturally sought my viewpoint. I tried to be neutral, feared to give myself away. This certainly was no ordinary interview. It was almost like a discussion. Dr. O'Hara pleasant, relaxed. Now it was almost over. I felt that I had shielded myself quite well and impressed Dr. O'Hara with my ability to be his secretary. Did I think that I could teach shorthand two hours an evening? I thought I could. Very well the job was mine. Then very casually came a stunning question: "If you don't mind, Miss Robbins, tell me, how radical are you?"

At this point the shock was more than I could take. So after all I have given myself away, in some way, by some remark. It was useless to go on fencing. I couldn't go on pretending. Yes, Dr. O'Hara, I am quite the radical, one who believes in the changing of our social and economic order. And on and on I went with my exposition. And then waited to be told that I was not the person for the job. But Dr. O'Hara only smiled as he listened. Well, I had a right to my political and economic theories. He was sure they would not affect my capacity for the job. I would begin on the following Monday.

My feeling as I left was one of resolve. It seemed improbable, for all of Dr. O'Hara's broad-mindedness, that I could fit into the Knights of Columbus School. There was also the resistance born of the rejection of association with activities sponsored by religious groups. So through the weekend playing with Vita and conscious of how much I needed the job, I nevertheless decided against taking it. I wrote a rather longish letter to Dr. O'Hara, discussing the social difficulties that might arise for one of such different background as I, as well as perhaps generally embarrassing situations for both. I felt that the job was not for me.

The letter, sent special delivery, reached Dr. O'Hara on Monday morning. He telephoned me at the Placement Bureau and asked if I could see him when I was through there. He wanted to discuss my letter. His reception of me was so completely genial and our discussion was so completely frank that I began to regret having sent the letter. "But Miss Robbins, I have not committed you to anything that would interfere with your political opinions," he argued. "There need be no question there. Only one thing I would ask of you: that you carry on no open agitation in the office. Can you accept that?"

I have never had a happier job. Between Dr. O'Hara and myself there was mutual respect and complete cooperation. My teaching experience was also very rewarding. There was little turnover in my classes. And when the term ended my students presented me with flowers and a gift—a silk umbrella.

As the school year was drawing to a close, Dr. O'Hara told the staff that funds were precarious and the school may not reopen next year. In May this was confirmed. And so once again I would soon be looking for another job. During the eight months with the school (I gave up my part-time job after the second month) I was able, by living very frugally, to pay off some debts and to save about $200. And I began

to dream of spending the summer with Vita and away from Washington.

During the months in Washington there was desultory correspondence between Ben and myself. He professed to miss me, begged for reconciliation, wanted to come to Washington. I resisted it. Nothing would be gained. I would again be swept into a storm of unhappiness: the resentment, the bitterness. He was forever the idler, an emotional and economic sponge. No, I would not have him disturb my existence and with that the existence of Vita.

But he came without my consent. And once again for a brief day or two there was rekindled warmth. We visited with Vita together. I remember Mrs. Stilson observing Ben quietly for a few minutes as I introduced him, and without a word walking out of the room. "The man hasn't a grain of sincerity in his make-up," she later told Marie Kravitz. It was hard for me to take this and the obvious avoidance of him by the Zasulys. On the third day of his visit he broke out in his typical nasty jealousy: Isidore Lattman was in love with me. I was living at the Zasulys because of "that cock-eyed little runt," etc., etc. We were in a restaurant at the time. I was too furious to speak. Shaking with anger I left the table, went to the women's restroom, and there broke down. I returned to the table and paid the dinner check. Outside and struggling not to break down again I asked him not to come home with me, unless to pick up his suitcase and leave.

We rode in silence to the house and went through the hall to my room to avoid anyone. He picked up his things. I gave him the money for the railroad fare to New York. My anger was gone and I was weeping. We shook hands and parted in silence.

MATILDA WENT TO WASHINGTON, D.C., WHERE HER closest friend, Marie Hourwich, now married to Aaron Kravitz, and a recent mother, welcomed her. Like Matilda, Marie was a Russian Jewish émigré. Her father, Isaac Hourwich, an economist and lawyer, was a Socialist who had been arrested and imprisoned in St. Petersburg for "hostility to the government" in 1879. Fleeing the country following his release, he abandoned his wife and four children when Marie was about seven years old. He eventually immigrated to the United States, where he worked in a variety of government jobs as a translator and statistician. Having divorced Marie's mother, he remarried, fathering five more children. He was a labor activist and an ardent Zionist.

Eventually Marie, who was from an educated middle-class background, also immigrated to the United States and found government work on the labor surveys where Matilda was her assistant. The two women developed a deep and lasting friendship. They were close, but in Matilda's statement that "she wasn't too eager to take a job," and earlier in the memoir when she suggests that Marie was self-conscious about her Russian-accented speech, Matilda acknowledges, with perhaps a grain of bitterness, the social and economic disparity that allowed Marie a measure of privilege. Regardless of talents and skills, self-conscious about her educational deficits, and financially self-supporting, Matilda's life was precarious. Marie chose not to work; Matilda had no such choice.

Matilda was faced with the difficulties of a wage-earning mother—the childcare arrangements, the social isolation, the twenty-four-hour job of worker and mother, with no support from husband or family. Through friendship she devised strategies to alleviate her burdens. And the friendships she developed in this part of her life were based on mutual understanding of the individual struggles of single women, where class also plays a role.

Matilda found herself in a new milieu—more middle class, more Jewish. Music, literature, and conversation were the social currency here, politics and activism less significant. She doesn't tell us much about her move from the Kravitz apartment, leaving Vita in the care of Mrs. Stilson, except that it was closer to her job. How difficult it must have been to see her daughter only on weekends.

Life with Max and Sonia Zasuly was congenial, and Matilda was able to save a little money. The other boarder, Isidore Lattman, whom Ben saw as a romantic rival, does not seem to have been attractive to Matilda. In fact, although she describes him as "likeable," she also calls him a braggart and "short, swarthy, near-sighted"—Jewish stereotypes. Ben's hatred of Lattman seemed tinged with anti-Semitism.

Lattman did obtain the degree he was working toward when Matilda knew him and became a radiologist for Children's Hospital of the District of Columbia with a teaching practice at Georgetown University. Among his famous patients were Supreme Court Justice Oliver Wendell Holmes and Treasury Secretary Andrew Mellon. Matilda thought him to be in love with Sonia. They shared a love of music, and Sonia must have fallen in love with Isidore, as his obituary lists a stepson with the surname "Sasuly."

Matilda took a few, but significant, jobs with institutions she opposed: the Guaranty Trust Company, a bank, and later the AFL. During her time in Washington, D.C., she worked for Catholics (where she could have felt no affinity)—the Knights of Columbus.

Working for Dr. O'Hara was surprisingly satisfying. Dr. Frank O'Hara was a founder of the Rehabilitation School, a project of the Knights of Columbus and the Catholic University, organized to educate and train ex-servicemen and -women, as Matilda says. Returning from World War I, these people embraced the opportunities offered, and Matilda obviously enjoyed her interaction with them. O'Hara was a liberal, a scholar who received his doctorate in economics at Berlin University with a thesis analyzing Henry George's single-tax theory. Many progressives were attracted to George's theories. At the Rehabilitation School Matilda was respected and offered responsibility and autonomy, and she left greatly disappointed when the Catholic University of America, its parent, closed the school. O'Hara assumed a professorship in economics at Catholic University following the closure. Matilda sought another job.

Ben continued to visit, but Matilda finally insisted that he leave after a series of offensive and violent conflicts with her in the presence of her friends. One more time, she gave him money for his rail fare.

15 BALLARDVALE, GREENWICH VILLAGE, COS COB, ST. LOUIS

The school was closing. Dr. O'Hara said he had exhausted all avenues for obtaining funds for the next year. He was very unhappy about the situation. Even if by some fortuitous circumstance the school could be reopened, he could not again assemble as good a staff as he had. We parted in friendship and with regret.

During the last six weeks of my stay in Washington letters from Ben kept pouring in. He was now in Lawrence again. He had no regular job, but some living expenses from the union. Such regrets, such self-abnegation, such pleas for forgiveness he sent. We must try again, he wrote. No, our love was not dead; it would never die . . . perhaps . . . again stirrings in me.

He knew I was planning to leave Washington in June and find some place in the country. Would I let him find a place for me? Somewhere not too far from Lawrence, where he could see us occasionally during the summer? He was looking at ads in the papers, and he sent me clippings with locations and prices. There was a place at Ballardvale, right on the river, pleasant and cheap. There was swimming and a rowboat, and above all it was near to Dedham, where the Sacco-Vanzetti trial was in progress. Fred Moore was lawyer for the defense.

I was very tired. I wanted more than anything else to have the summer with Vita in the country. I didn't know how I would do it on the little money I had saved—perhaps with the greatest economy. Where would I go after the summer? I didn't know, and I didn't want to think. My friends hoped that I would change my mind. Sonia and Marie were both aware of the unhappy relationship with Ben. They had seen us together during those days in Washington. Marie had known other times and other incidents in our affair. "Would you not consider finding a summer place in Takoma Park, or somewhere else near Washington?" she asked. "Perhaps we could share a place." They knew I had very little money. They would help, if I needed it. But I was pulled otherwise . . . again otherwise.

I settled on Ballardvale and sent the money for the season's rent to Ben who offered to get the place ready for us. He met us in Boston, and we went out there together. The little house was small and shabby and in poor repair, but there was grass for Vita to run on and the river's edge to play with sand and pebbles. She was healthy and happy. I watched her at play by the hour, sitting or lying outdoors. There was the daily swim in the river, the daily chores, the drifting down in the old rowboat every other day to get groceries and the newspaper at the village. Living was easy.

Ben stayed a week and left to do his work in Lawrence, but at the end of the next week he was back. There was nothing more to do in Lawrence. There was dissension in the union, he had much opposition, and he wouldn't go on with the activities. He hoped later to get something to do on the Sacco-Vanzetti case, do some speaking, traveling. But if not that, he might get a job with a stock company. Always he dreamed of a job with a stock company, but only twice through all the years that I knew him did he actually have such work—no more than several months altogether, but through the years he lived in the green room.

I was glad to have him back. Love, not altogether dead, begged for another chance. We were both excited by the Sacco-Vanzetti trial which was going on. Ben made many trips to Dedham, and I spent one whole day in the courtroom where I saw and heard both men from their cages.

Early in July Ben brought Jane, who was then about 12, to stay with us. Of the three girls I liked her best. A delicate and gentle girl, she gained weight, swam a lot with her father, and had a happy vacation. She left in August to visit with her mother who was still living and working in Washington. In September she returned to Fairhope where Mrs. Johnson continued to support the three girls on funds she raised yearly.

We celebrated Vita's second birthday on July 31st. This was the first and only birthday at which Ben was present. We had a picnic party and rowed up and down the river. It was a happy day. I can still see Vita dancing and cavorting: red cheeks, sturdy limbs, hair blowing.

My small savings were running out. The rent was paid to the first of September, but there was hardly enough for a month's food left.

Ben had contributed nothing to living expenses. He did get a few dollars somewhere, I never knew where, which he spent on bringing Jane up, and he bought her shoes. I bought her a dress and some underwear. He had no money for her trip to Washington. Her mother sent part of the fare, and I made up the rest.

In mid-August Sonia Zasuly came to spend a week with me. She saw at once what the situation was and insisted on buying a week's food, a most generous supply. We ate better during that week than during the entire stay. Sonia was a warm and understanding person. I was glad to have at least one friend, one visitor, after so many weeks in Ballardvale. But Ben made the visit difficult. Although Sonia had made him welcome as a guest when he came to Washington, he showed her no courtesy and at times was downright nasty. He quarreled with both of us repeatedly. At mealtimes he would disappear or eat in sulky silence. When at the end of her stay Isidore Lattman came to accompany her to New York, Ben broke into a rage and heaped insults on both of them.

Violently angry, I verbally attacked him for his hypocrisy, irresponsibility, and lack of ordinary decency. He grabbed me by the wrist and threw me against the wall. I heard a gasp from Sonia and Isidore's "No, no!" as they fled the room, and Ben bolted out of the house. They stayed an hour or so, until the car they ordered to take them to the junction arrived. I could not talk, and they respected my mood. Their small talk helped [keep] me from breaking down. That came after they left.

I was in a fever all night. I sat beside Vita's crib and wept, steeped in the misery of ugly memories. It had all happened before, two, three, four times, but never before other people. This would be the last time.

At daybreak I heard Ben in the kitchen. Then I heard him go out again. Vita was awake, talking. It was morning. I took her up, kissed and hugged her madly, and struggled against tears. I gave her breakfast and drank strong coffee. The air was sultry. We walked down to the river in our bathing suits. It was only midmorning and already warm enough to bathe. I sat down on the bank, watching Vita bring sand and pebbles. Then I saw Ben swimming toward us from the opposite bank. My first impulse was to pick up Vita and run. I couldn't bear his presence. But I sat speechless. He spoke to Vita, asked her if she wanted to go in the water. She came to me, took my hand, and pulled me toward the river. He took her other hand. I tried not to break out in laughter, in tears, hysteria. The water helped me. Vita was splashing as Ben was holding her up, and I swam along. Enough. I took her in and we walked to the house, leaving Ben sitting on the bank.

Late that day, while Vita took a long afternoon nap and I was sitting outside reading, Ben sat down beside me. He had been out of the house for hours, and I had been avoiding him. Now he wanted to talk. He wanted to tell me how he regretted his violence. He was overcome by the feeling that Sonia would influence me to return to Washington, and that "cockeyed bastard, Lattman," him he hated. Once again, could I forgive? He loved me. He will try. But I knew it was hopeless. I tried. How I tried! But I would not again. It had finally come to an end.

The rent on the place had only another week to run. I insisted that Ben leave at once. I made plans to go to New York. During the summer I was asked to accept a job as organizer for the Office Workers Union, at that time called Accountants, Bookkeepers and Stenographers Union (AFL). I delayed the answer. I did not want to live in New York, especially not with Vita, and I did not want to work for the AFL. It was the only offer of a job I had had, and it would permit me to return to workers' organizing. So I accepted.

Little did I realize at the time the extent and influence of the Communist Party machine. Little did I anticipate the conquest and the wrecking methods Communist members of unions employed. This was, after all, an AFL local, conservative and insignificant in membership. The few active members, Socialists mostly, tried to get some life into the union, to tackle the difficult problem of organizing New

York's office workers, tens of thousands of them working for low wages under deplorable conditions. I was to learn quickly what the Commies wanted.

I borrowed money to get to New York. I borrowed more to pay the first month's rent which was $100. My weekly union wage of $35 was to start on September first. My brother Bob, just turned 20, and now a proofreader and a member of the International Typographical Union, would live with us and share expenses. We had three large rooms on the street-level floor and two on the second floor, one a very large front room and the other the parlor of an old brownstone house. This room my friend Helen Boyd took at $50 a month. I still needed to find someone to look after Vita while I was at work. It would mean $12 or $15 a week, and I would not get paid for two weeks. We had hardly enough for food and carfare.

I had heard of Greenwich House Nursery for working mothers, not too far from our 17 Charles Street address. I decided to take Vita there until I could get someone to take care of her at home. There was a little enclosed yard in the rear of our place which had been what determined me to take it—the yard, and the convenience of the place to the office.

A new job, a child, a home to make for her—the days and evenings were crowded. The load was a heavy one, but I was happy. I was happy to have Vita, happy to be spared the destroying times with Ben, content to be doing the kind of work I liked, and glad to have friends and fellow workers around me.

Each morning, after taking Vita to the nursery, I would go to my job. At 6 or 6:30 each evening we would come home where I would get dinner, bathe her, put her to bed, then finish the necessary chores—dishes, laundry, tidying, and so forth. In union work there are evening calls to be made, and often meetings. I needed help to relieve me for these, but I could not afford to pay a housekeeper. The care at the nursery was not satisfactory. There was an incidence of intestinal illness among thousands of children, and for the first time Vita was ill. Now

there was a real emergency—a crisis. Somehow we managed with help from Helen, who
gave a few hours, and Bob, who was working
swing shift. At the end of a week I had found
a girl to come in five days a week, from 2 p.m.
to 6 p.m., for $12. In the mornings Ella Reeve
Bloor's daughter-in-law, Chris Ware, and I
arranged to share the cost of childcare at my
place. A girl who lived with the Wares looked
after Vita and the Ware's daughter, Judy Ware,
who was about Vita's age. The babysitter was
intelligent and pleasant with the children. My
house with its little yard was more desirable
than the Ware's third-floor apartment. The
children could be outdoors and have a safe
play area, rare advantages in New York, especially for those of small income.

The union work was difficult. The membership was small and
composed largely of people with decided political opinions and sharp
political differences. It was only four years after the Russian Revolution, and the followers of the Bolsheviks were already assuming pre-
rogatives in unions and becoming continually more aggressive.

New York had a quarter million office workers—in banks, in commerce, in department stores, in factories. The union had a membership of about 400, the only AFL local in the vast unorganized field. I
had never before done labor organizing in New York City, nor among
office workers. The whole field was new. The problems were different
from those of textile workers, pottery workers, cigar-makers, and auto
workers with whom I had worked before. Office workers, unlike factory workers, did not live near their places of work. It was a physical
impossibility to reach them in their homes, scattered through New
York, Brooklyn, and the Bronx.

We devised a program of education: to start a monthly bulletin, to print leaflets for distribution at office buildings, banks, and so forth, to hold weekly meetings, to use informed members in seeking out leads, and to make individual contacts. Quite a program!

I worked with an executive committee and an action committee composed of a larger number of members. "The Office Worker," a four-page printed sheet, came out; leaflets were distributed; the meetings went off to a good start. Union offices need evening hours. This immediately entailed difficulties for me. I had to be home in time to let the housekeeper go, not later than six. It meant making special arrangements for meeting nights, both regular and occasional. It meant paying the girl extra for the hours, now and then a special sitter. This strain was added to the already heavy load, but I found contentment in the weekends with Vita.

And there were friends and associates: Socialists and Wobblies, some of whom were coming out of Leavenworth, having served three and four years since the IWW Chicago trial of 1917. My home became something of a center for them. My life was full.

Before long Ben arrived. He came one day as I was sitting down to dinner with my brother and a friend, Art Shields. I received him coolly, although I did ask him to eat with us. He said he had come to New York to look for work on the stage. He had some promising interviews. He was staying with someone on Patchin Place (a Bohemian slum) for a few days but would have to find a place to live. He talked and talked about his differences and difficulties with the people in the One Big Union. No one appreciated his efforts, or his skill as an organizer. Art realized my discomfort and tension. He got up to go and asked Ben if he would like to come along and meet some "interesting" people. They might like to hear about some of his experiences with the OBU. And they left together to my great relief.

Bob and I talked. He said I was in for more trouble, and well I knew it. But this time I knew that I would not break down, would not accept any association. When [Ben] came again I was alone. He began his old pleas. He would accept any condition, if only I would let him come

back. No. Everything was over between us. My decision was final. I wanted to be let alone . . . with Vita . . . with my work. When I asked him to leave I saw his old violence rising and I was afraid. How to get rid of him? I was hoping for someone to come in. The telephone rang. Yes, I remembered the committee meeting. Yes, I would have the draft of the leaflet ready. It could go to the printer in the morning.

The meeting was for another night, but I said that I expected the members in an hour. I had some work to do before then. Would he go? No, he would like to stay. He wouldn't bother anybody. I insisted on his going. He began to shout, to hurl insults, "You IWW bitch! You AFL whore!" I opened the door and stepped outside. Just then the owner who lived on the top floor appeared. Ben beat a hasty retreat. I did not see him again for years.

It was a rewarding year in some ways and in some ways very difficult. The union work was demanding more time and energy than

I could give. Union organization always means much evening work. The office needs to be open for contacts, for the collection of dues, for committee meetings. This part was a great problem for me. I could not afford to pay a housekeeper to live in, nor did I have the room for one. I was getting $35 a week, and even with Helen paying $40 a month for her room and my brother Bob contributing his share, I found it difficult to pay the $12 a week for the five days of service. But it was rewarding to know that Vita was well cared for, and I was happy to have her with me.

I also participated in interesting and stimulating work for our political prisoners, IWWs and Socialists who were beginning to come out of prison. Many of them came and went through New York, and my house was a stopover. The Political Prisoners Defense Committee of which I was secretary used my house as its address.

I was young, attractive, and interesting to more than one of the radicals, but none affected my emotional life enough to form even a temporary attachment. Helen Boyd, ever ready for a romantic or a sexual experience, taunted me for being a "Puritan," which was rather absurd. Casual sex affairs had no appeal for me. And I wasn't in love with any of the men who came and went and with whom I had common intellectual and social interests. "You keep your arms around the movement," quipped one in disappointment. I was no doubt too self-contained, and I kept my arms around Vita.

The union work proceeded relatively well during the first months. The office, records, files, books, etc. were in order. We were issuing a bulletin and later a printed four-page sheet, "The Office Worker." This was a new, all-inclusive name on the masthead. Below it was the official name of the union: Bookkeepers, Stenographers and Accountants Union (AFL). Since the union membership included typists, file clerks, and other types of office workers, the union voted to adopt the new name. There was some objection later from the AFL state secretary to what he considered an arbitrary definition in the name "office worker." This was characteristic of the craft union conservatism of the AFL. Even the venture of a more meaningful name for a union was questioned. But beyond our presuming to change our name, our union was suspect for its radicalism. Most of the members came from the offices of the garment workers' unions: the International Ladies' Garment Worker's Union, Amalgamated Clothing Workers, Millinery Workers, and others. Many were Socialists. We were still untroubled by Communists.

I worked very hard, but results were unrewarding. The job was too big for one person. I could not even begin to cover one-tenth of the field. We carried on as well as we could, mainly in the printing and distribution of leaflets, issues of "The Office Worker." But here, as only a small accretion of members, the revenue from dues was too small to allow for an expansive campaign. The state AFL received our per capita tax of several hundred members, but it was uninterested in broadening our activities either through financial or moral support.

I had dropped my membership in the Socialist Party some years before but remained a Socialist. It was not too long after I came to the union that the Communist members, of whom there were only a few, began to show their designs. They knew that I had no party affiliation. They knew my record as an IWW organizer, and they began to solicit me. If they could win the organizer to their side, they could naturally exert greater influence. They found me very difficult, indeed an adversary. Apparently they expected something else.

A number of IWW members and some who had been prominent in the organization had joined the Communist Party, and party hucksters were deployed to draw others into it. There was flattery of one's record, implied power offered, suggestions of their importance as representatives of the Workers' Fatherland, offers of jobs. There was always a frenetic search for likely material for the growing Communist movement. Haywood was now in Russia, and reports were widespread about the important role he was playing there, the recognition and honors that were conferred on him.

Most of my fellow members in the union were sincerely interested in the growth of the union. The Communists, only a mere handful at the time, were in the field to ply the party line and to solicit members. I must have surprised them by the complete rejection of their advances. I saw Haywood in Washington in the spring, only a few days before he jumped his bail and left for Russia, a captive of the Communists. I knew well the shock his betrayal [gave to] his fellow workers in the prisons who trusted him [during] the famous Chicago mass trial. He alone was offered bail, $20,000 of which was yet to be paid off by the IWW. I had only contempt for Haywood's act, but the CP was now promoting him, holding him up as an example for others to follow. They soon discovered where I stood on this question and others.

Through the months that followed the difficulties grew. The union hall became a battleground for the political bickering between the Socialists and the Communists. Resolutions! There was always some resolution that led to hours of contention. The line-up was pretty well defined: Socialists on one side, Communists on the other—literally on opposites sides of the room. The succeeding months sharpened the internal debate, as the succeeding years were to continue to show— Socialists and Communists embattled.

The union was an unsuccessful undertaking. I felt more and more the difficulties and the futility of carrying on. After eight months I resigned, and immediately the Communists "captured" the union. It was a pattern that repeated itself for some years in many unions. Some were wrecked, some survived to fight another day.

In June 1922, I found a place for Vita in the country, at the home of a woman in Wilton, Connecticut. She also boarded five other children whose parents I knew. Vita was the youngest and much beloved. One of the children was Walta Karsner, three or four years older than Vita.

It was difficult to get to Wilton, especially on a Sunday when I went to see her there. The train from New York did not go through to the little town, and there was only a short branch line with very uncertain service. I went every other week, and often every week. It was a great joy to see my beautiful child, well and happy and loved by all.

We had a birthday party for her there when she was three. I gave her a doll with a china head, hands, and feet, which some weeks later met with disaster and was buried with great ceremony at the end of the lot, near the fence and under a tree. I bought Vita another doll, of course, but the first one was remembered for a long time.

My new job was with the ACW's *Advance*. The ACW had set up the Russian-American Industrial Corporation (RAIC) to provide a million or more for the development of the Russian clothing industry. Sidney Hillman had gone to Russia and was enthusiastic about building up the industry and the part his union might play in it. Jacob Potofsky, then the secretary-treasurer, headed RAIC. My special job was publicity for the stock promotion campaign and to write a special feature column under the head of RAIC.

The editor of *Advance* was Horace Kallen, a former philosophy professor at Harvard. There was much questioning among the staff about Dr. Kallen's suitability for the job. He had no practical experience in journalism, nor in the labor movement. He was known among educators as a philosopher of standing, and he was a political liberal. He was incongruous in the editor's job and depended on the staff for opinions as well as practical work, but Hillman chose a prominent Harvard professor for the job (for the prestige that he

lent it). It was entirely in keeping with Hillman's rising power and his intent to fill the ACW with the glitter of personnel with college degrees. Though he was himself without any formal education, he was filled with pretense and aspired to be an important public figure. He surrounded himself with men who taught him and wrote his speeches and who raised him to the eventual stature of labor statesman. Dr. Kallen would be too innocent to know why he was hired for the job, but it was clear to me that his prestige was Hillman's capital investment in self-promotion.

Dr. Kallen was a gentle soul, sentimental and unsure of what he wanted for the paper. My own job was rather independent, having to do with the collection of material for the weekly column of RAIC, sending out press releases on the progress of the venture, and taking care of a large correspondence. On occasion Dr. Kallen discussed with me the possible use of some articles on my experience as an organizer in the textile industry, but nothing came of it. I gathered that mention of the IWW was taboo. Only once did I flare up at him for permitting a cartoon on the front page of a May Day issue, extolling the virtue of saving by presenting a well-dressed man who saved and a ragged one who didn't, sitting opposite one another on a park bench. Dr. Kallen could see nothing objectionable in publishing the cartoon in *Advance*.

My job on the *Advance* lasted several months. RAIC wasn't doing well, and the whole scheme was eventually written off as a loss.

During this time I had a house in Cos Cob commuting to New York five days a week. I had a housekeeper who came every morning in time for me to catch the 8:11 and was ready to leave the minute I stepped into the house at 6:15.

The weekends were busy with many household tasks. In cold weather there were two stoves to keep going; coal to carry in, ashes to take out. But there were lovely short walks in the snow, and building snowmen in the back yard, and pulling Vita on a sled and reading to her. It was a happy time. When spring came and the small sound inlet permitted a rowboat, my brother Bob, who came out weekends, would row and we would swim. They were happy months.

But soon I had to look for another job. Fortunately one turned up. The Co-operative Society where I had a contact was asked by the Central States Co-op, with headquarters in E. St. Louis, [Illinois], to find someone to work in its educational department. This was the clearinghouse for a chain of Consumer Co-ops, scattered between S. Illinois and N. Missouri, in the coal mining region. The co-ops were organized and supported financially by the United Mine Workers of America. I took the job and left for St. Louis in August 1923.

I liked the work. It was interesting writing educational releases, dealing with correspondence, and coediting the *Co-operator*. Vita and I had pleasant room and board with the Burton family where there was a child Vita's age. She spent the morning in private kindergarten and was brought home after lunch where she had a nap and then playmates in the afternoon. We took walks in the park nearby and sometimes went to the zoo or to see a puppet show. The office of the co-op was in E. St. Louis, and travelling across the Mississippi back and forth each day was tiresome. My evenings, after dinner and some time with Vita, were generally spent at home. The Burtons were kind and pleasant people, but we had little in common, except our

children. Also, I was not in as good health as I usually had been. The climate, miasmic in the summer and fall, affected me badly. Besides Warriner, who was the manager of the *Co-operator*, and his wife, I made no friends. But I had Vita and I was not discontented.

THE MEMOIR ENDS HERE.

Perhaps the ferment over the trial of Sacco and Vanzetti drew Matilda and Ben together once again. One of the great trials of the early twentieth century, it has long been regarded as a miscarriage of justice. Nicola Sacco and Bartolomeo Vanzetti were on trial for the murder of a paymaster in Braintree, Massachusetts. Most people on the left believed that they were on trial for being anarchists and immigrants. Criminalizing Sacco's and Vanzetti's origins and politics was believed to be the real intent of the trial, not proving they were guilty of murder.

Wobblies and Socialists were deeply involved in the trial where their comrade, counsel Fred Moore, was in charge of the defense. It was said that his inexperience as a trial lawyer in Massachusetts and the defendants' distrust of him were at issue, and he was ultimately replaced. Matilda told us that she was convinced of Vanzetti's innocence, and after meeting him she was greatly moved. Her impressions of the prison and her observations of the court proceedings were published in the *Industrial Pioneer* (July 1924), but she kept no copies of the text. I found it reproduced in Joyce Kornbluh's *Rebel Voices*.* Sacco she found less sympathetic, perhaps because he didn't trust Moore or members of the defense committee. Matilda thought it was possible that he was involved in the murder, and according to some accounts Moore also doubted his innocence. The trial and appeals dragged on for years, and finally the two were executed to international outcry.

*Joyce L. Kornbluh, ed., *Rebel Voices: An IWW Anthology* (1964), with a new introduction by Fred Thompson (Chicago: Charles H. Kerr, 1998).

Meanwhile Matilda had the summer with Vita, long days outside, the river, fresh air, trees, and grass. Ben assigned his daughter Jane to Matilda's care, and Vita's sister was warmly welcomed, but finances were tight. Ben seems not to have contributed much, if anything. Matilda paid the rent, bought the food and a dress and underwear for Jane. Her friend Sonia visited from Washington and was appalled at the scant provisions, so Ben may have considered her generosity a rebuke. Perhaps the feeling of censure explains the violence that erupted and caused the final break.

Finally it was over. He did not appear in their lives again for more than a decade, and then only peripherally.

When Matilda eventually had to return to New York for work, the only job she could find was with the AFL, an organization she strongly opposed. But she had no choice, and if the politics were disagreeable the work was familiar. She is dismissive of Horace Kallen, who was a prominent liberal intellectual. Kallen was a Zionist who coined the term "cultural pluralism" and supported the idea that diversity strengthened society, an incongruous attitude for a supporter of a state exclusively for Jews. Matilda was an internationalist and an anti-Zionist. But her real criticism was for labor leaders who assumed the privileges of the ruling class. Sidney Hillman, head of the Amalgamated Clothing Workers of America and one of the founders of the CIO, was really the betrayer in Matilda's eyes. Hillman believed that labor should work with employers for stability, and even supported Taylorism. "Certainly, I believe in collaborating with the employers!" he is reported to have said. "That is what unions are for. I even believe in helping an employer function more productively. For then, we will have a claim to higher wages, shorter hours, and greater participation in the benefits of running a smooth industrial machine."* These

*"Garment Worker Expanded Union Ideals Beyond the Workplace," November 2009, Labor History Articles, American Postal Workers Union, AFL-CIO, https://www.apwu.org/labor-history-articles/garment-worker-expanded-union-ideals-beyond-workplace.

views were antithetical to Matilda's understanding of working-class solidarity.

Her denunciation of the Communist Party here ("the Commies") is retrospective. In fact, she says a little later, when she began to work for the Bookkeepers, Stenographers and Accountants Union, they were untroubled by Communists. When she arranged joint babysitting with the daughter-in-law of Ella Reeve Bloor, she had relationships with labor activists of many political shades and among people of diverse social classes. Bloor was a labor organizer known as "Mother Bloor" and a close friend of Eugene Debs, for whom Matilda had profound, lifelong admiration. Bloor, however, came to regard Debs as utopian and moved away from the Socialist Party.

The connection of the two young mothers, based on mutual need, must have been congenial and comradely. Cris Ware (Cris, not Chris—for Clarissa Smith Ware) was the wife of Harold Ware, Bloor's son. Both Bloor and Harold Ware had been Socialists until two years before Matilda's childcare arrangement with the Wares. In

1919 mother and son joined the newly formed Communist Labor Party, which later became the CPUSA. Both Bloor and Ware became important functionaries in the Communist Party, and Cris Ware also assumed roles of responsibility in the 1920s.

Harold Ware, a federal employee in the Department of Agriculture, was in later years a suspected member of a group of spies in government known as the "Ware Group," according to Whittaker Chambers. Chambers was a Soviet spy, who later renounced Communism and testified against Alger Hiss during his espionage trial, and implicated a number of government employees, including Ware.

Matilda regarded Haywood's defection and

forfeiture of bail as an act of treachery against his comrades and the Socialists. Mary Marcy was particularly betrayed, as she had mortgaged her house to guarantee Haywood's bond; she committed suicide soon after Haywood left for Russia.

Matilda claims to have rejected any amorous associations once she bid a final farewell to Ben: "I kept my arms around Vita." My mother told a different story. After Matilda left New York, when she moved to St. Louis, there was a period where, according to Vita, Matilda and Fred Moore probably were romantically involved.

Exhausted and embattled, Matilda changed jobs and decided to solve her pressing childcare problems by placing Vita in a boarding situation in Connecticut. She mentions Walta Karsner, the daughter of her friend Rose Karsner. At the time that Matilda was writing the memoir I was probably in junior high school, and Walta's daughter, Lorna Ross, was one of my best friends. Rose Karsner was married to James P. Cannon, a Trotskyist and the founder of the Socialist Workers Party in the United States. Walta (she was named Walta Whitman Karsner) was not Cannon's daughter, but Cannon assumed the role of grandfather to my friend Lorna. I knew the grandparents as "Nana" and "Bam." Bam had part of one of his thumbs missing; it was the first time I remember seeing such a disfigurement, so it remains part of my mental picture of him.

Once again Matilda changed childcare arrangements and jobs. The process of juggling work, commuting, childcare, and domestic duties was extraordinarily difficult. Along with her work as an organizer, evening meetings, producing publicity, and writing a regular column for *Advance*, Matilda continued to write fictionalized stories and poetry. In 1927, several years after the period represented here, now living in Los Angeles, she wrote a piece, "From the Life of a Wage Earning Mother," describing her struggle to balance the demands of a job with those of motherhood. She submitted the article to the *Nation* magazine with the byline "Anonymous." Fifty years later Vita submitted the same piece to *Redbook* magazine noting, "Today my

daughter is a young mother struggling with many of the same problems that her grandmother faced." Vita also said this about Matilda:

> To make a deliberate decision to be an unwed mother is no great
> distinction in 1977. But in 1919 it was an act of enormous cour-
> age. Now, perhaps, my mother would not find it necessary to
> be anonymous nor fail to mention why she "had no husband to
> depend on." Attitudes, if not circumstances, have changed. But
> in 1927 she was a social worker in a private agency and used a Mrs.
> before her maiden name although she had never married. To have
> a father for her child without a husband for herself was also a
> deliberate choice. From childhood I was aware of these facts and
> unaware of any stigma attached to them. But my mother obvi-
> ously protected her job and her child by the use of Mrs. and the
> public appearance of a "divorced" woman rather than an "unwed
> mother" (I'm sure she would have felt less compromise had the
> Ms. of today been acceptable then).
>
> Her title and some of the prose sounds a bit quaint now. But
> Matilda Robbins was not at all "quaint." She was a feminist, a
> labor organizer and a rebel. In her published writing she was
> essentially a polemicist and contributed columns to radical papers
> to the end of her life.

Fifty years later Matilda's article was again rejected. It is published
in full in the appendix to this book.

Accepting the job at the Central States Co-op in East St. Louis was
the beginning of Matilda's move westward. She may have gone to St.
Louis in the company of Fred Moore, but Matilda and Vita's trip from
St. Louis to California when Vita was six was certainly with Moore.
Vita vividly recalled traveling through the Columbia River Gorge in
his Model T Ford. Matilda had intended to settle in San Francisco,
but it was July when they arrived, foggy and cold, usual weather in
San Francisco at that time of year, but not the California climate that
she expected. So they went on to Southern California, where Fred

Moore had family. Shortly after settling in California, Matilda wrote a short sketch called "Following the Gasoline Trail" about travelers they met in the tourist camps where the three stayed for the weeks that they spent driving to California. Many of the migrants were large families traveling in barely roadworthy vehicles, subsisting on scant rations, and hoping to find work in the west.

Through California's Central Valley they continued to Los Angeles where Matilda lived for most of the rest of her life.

Matilda Reading Outside 1950

MATILDA'S LIFE FOLLOWING THE
EVENTS DESCRIBED IN HER MEMOIR

It is unclear when Taube Gitel Rabinowitz became Matilda Gertrude Robbins, but her naturalization certificate uses the anglicized version of her name, and it was the name she used for most of her life.

Matilda and Vita moved to Los Angeles in 1925. Her memoir ends when she is thirty-eight, the chronological midpoint of her life. It's difficult to reconstruct the details of the last half of her life, because what ephemeral records existed—letters, diaries, and photos—were lost in a burglary of my parents' home in 1991. What I know about her life during those years is what I remember her telling me, what I observed, or what others told me about her, especially tales from my mother. Matilda's young comrade Harry Siitonen was editor of the Los Angeles *Socialist Newsletter* where Matilda penned a monthly editorial called "On The Left." Several years ago, Harry, then in his eighties, sent me copies of her articles, always placed in the far left column of the sheet under the byline "Barb." For many years she wrote also for the *Industrial Worker*, published by the IWW in Chicago.

Matilda lived and supported Vita on her salary as a social worker for a Jewish welfare agency. In those days one didn't need any specific certification to be a social worker. She was hired because, although an autodidact, she was educated, and she spoke Yiddish. Ironically, she was given a caseload of Sephardic immigrants, who spoke Ladino, not Yiddish, so she went to night school and studied Spanish to communicate with them. The family name on her mother's side was Schpanier, and Matilda looked Mediterranean; in Los Angeles she was often mistaken for Mexican.

She was determined to get the best education for her daughter that she could find. From the early grades, Vita was enrolled in the UCLA teachers' training school. Matilda found scholarship placement for Vita, for two or three years in middle school and high school, at a progressive boarding school in San Diego run by Daisy Lee Worcester, a Communist, former social worker, and writer. There were several other teachers at the school, but Daisy taught math and Latin, the two subjects that Matilda engaged a tutor to help her learn when she thought she would attend college. Vita went a year or two to Thomas Starr King Jr. High, and she graduated from John Marshall High School in Los Angeles, both of which I also attended.

Winifred Heath's son, Brian, also attended the Worcester school. Winifred and Matilda certainly met among Socialists in Bridgeport, where Brian was born in 1913. Brian was, like Vita, the child of an unmarried, progressive woman. Originally from England, Winifred was Anna Strunsky's typist and became her friend.* Matilda probably met Strunsky through Winifred, and these two foreign-born women, Socialists, unmarried with children, working as typists and stenographers, remained lifelong friends. Brian Heath was the cofounder, with his wife Edith, of Heath Ceramics, a highly regarded, award-winning pottery in California.

Matilda told no one, when her daughter was a student at UCLA or ever, that Aaron Kravitz, Marie Hourwich's husband, helped pay tuition, books, and living expenses for Vita. Many friends helped Matilda and her daughter thrive. It was the Socialist ethic and an example

---

* Heath and Strunsky's friendship is noted in James Boylan, *Revolutionary Lives: Anna Strunsky & William English Walling* (Amherst: University of Massachusetts Press, 1998), 212.

of the way, without husband or family, relationships were formed that were mutually supportive and took the place of family.

Vita felt the absence of a father always. After Ben left, Matilda destroyed all evidence of him—letters and photos. Sometimes she kept part of a group photograph, but scissored out the image of Ben. Vita knew very little about him and had no way of knowing even what he looked like. When Vita was fifteen or sixteen, Matilda agreed to a meeting. Vita was captivated. Ben courted her as he had so many women, sending notes, taking Vita to the theater, and sending amusing, inexpensive birthday gifts. One that Vita especially remembered was a parcel filled with hundreds of pennies, all stamped with the year of her birth, 1919. After these early meetings, Vita added to her surname, becoming Vita Robbins Légère. There is no record of how Matilda felt about this.

Matilda rejoined the SP, remained an active member and served as executive secretary of the Los Angeles Local from 1945 to 1947. She was a featured speaker at Socialist gatherings and she organized special events, such as the 1955 Eugene V. Debs Centennial celebration in Los Angeles. Her admiration for Debs never dimmed.

She and her fellow social workers at the Jewish Home for the Aged formed a union, and from some of her writings I gather that she nearly lost her job because of her political views. The Social Security Administration was created in 1935, and Matilda retired as early as she was eligible, only seven years later at the age of fifty-five. She continued to write and attend political meetings and events. She had a wide circle of friends, mostly women, all of them Socialists.

In Russia, Jews had been prohibited from owning, buying, or selling real estate. Thrifty and hardworking, Matilda bought and sold several properties in Los Angeles in the 1940s and 1950s. I spent summers with her in a charming little cottage she owned at Laguna Beach when I was seven or eight years old. There was a tiny well-tended garden with flowers and succulents, and we walked to the beach. In Los Angeles she lived in the apartment upstairs from us in the house she owned for a number of years. This property, in Echo Park, was built on a large lot, and in 1949 my parents began building a house behind our downstairs apartment. We lived in the new house for about a decade, and for most of that time Matilda lived upstairs in the front building (which has since burned down).

When Vita's relationship with her became difficult, Matilda sometimes moved out and rented an apartment in other parts of town, but not too far away. We saw her at least weekly. After World War II, in one of her periodic decampments, my grandmother moved out of the upstairs flat and advertised for tenants in the *Daily News*. The ad read, "1 bedroom apartment for rent. $50/mo. Nisei preferred."

Japanese Americans, interned during the war by the Roosevelt administration, were returning from the "relocation camps." The Communist Party had supported the U.S. government's decision to incarcerate persons of Japanese ancestry. My grandmother, who had been appalled by Executive Order 9066* and was disgusted by the Communist Party's support for Japanese imprisonment, wanted to do something to mitigate the racism and paranoia directed at citizens and legal permanent residents of Japanese descent, animus directed at them even after the war was over. A series of Nisei applicants responded to the ad, and over the next five years there were two or three small groups of Japanese American tenants at different times.

Matilda looked upon Israel as a theocracy and was opposed to the Zionist project. The notion of Jewish exceptionalism offended her democratic sensibilities and her internationalist beliefs. "How odd of God / To choose the Jews," she sometimes quipped. My grandmother saw the so-called Christian holidays as American rituals without particular religious significance to her or any of us. We celebrated Christmas with a tree and gifts and Easter with dyed eggs and candy, but I rarely saw the inside of a place of worship with my family, and I had no idea of Christian, or any other, religious iconography—what sig-

---

* Executive Order 9066, signed by President Franklin D. Roosevelt on February 19, 1942, authorized the secretary of war to prescribe military areas from which anyone could be excluded, clearing the way for deportation of Japanese Americans into internment camps.

nificance might attach to Easter eggs or Christmas trees. The families of my friends from school invited me to Evangelical and Methodist services. I had at least one friend whose mother attended séances and believed in astrology. The Catholic Church was always attractive with its stained glass, foreign language, incense, music, and kneeling, sitting, and standing rituals. For a few months when I was eight or nine, I attended Mass with my friends and learned the rituals and prayers of Catholic worship. My family left me to explore religion on my own. Anything I knew about Jewish mythology, lore, or culture was through friends and classmates. I was in college when I attended my first Seder.

We lived in Echo Park, a part of Los Angeles that was then home to Mexican immigrants, radicals, bohemians, and, as we said in those days, homosexuals. Neighbors on two contiguous properties on either side of us would have been categorized as such. I was a playmate of the daughters of one couple. I once made a comment that J and M's moms were lesbians, and Matilda shot back, "You don't know that!" Her experiences of being shunned for unconventional sexual behavior made her protective of these women leftists, also her friends. It's hard to imagine those days when we didn't know the word "gay" in that context and queers were considered "deviant."

I knew Matilda as a grandmother, and in that role she was loving and attentive. Even so, she was a fierce adversary in political discussions, and she argued knowledgably with anyone who disagreed with her, including me and my brother Eric. She clipped articles to bolster her arguments and was known to cut off a relationship if the disagreement was deep. She could be severe.

As she aged she became more and more melancholy, and her relationship with Vita deteriorated. When Matilda was in her early seventies, my parents moved our family from Los Angeles to Fresno. Matilda was bereft. Within eighteen months she had moved and bought a house near us, which my father maintained and repaired. Soon it became clear that Matilda would not be happy in a place where her only connections were with her small family. She did find a few friends in Fresno—Socialists and old Wobblies—but she was lonely. I was finishing high school and planning to go to college. I had a busy social life and boyfriends and was not as available as she would have liked. One night she took an overdose of sleeping pills. She called Vita to tell her what she had done saying, "Do with me what you wish." My parents called an ambulance. She was taken to the emergency room and soon after transferred for a short time to the mental hospital where my father, a psychologist, worked. She complained of her incarceration, "That's not what I wanted." However, she was quite a hit at the facility and made friends with another inmate who had succeeded my grandfather (on my father's side) as the pastor of one of the largest Protestant churches in Fresno. They argued about religion, and the reverend asked her how she would deal with the anger her views provoked. "Well," Matilda, the pacifist, replied, "I'd turn the other cheek." She knew the literature.

For a time, she returned to Los Angeles to stay with friends. I have her diary from this period, and it is terribly sad. She was restive and continued to be depressed. She was highly critical of her host, Sophie, who was still working and watched a lot of television in the evenings. Matilda was not a fan of television, but after all Sophie had spent eight hours in an office and she wanted some escape. Matilda had been alone in the house most of the day and wanted company.

Within a year, a plan was hatched to move to Berkeley where I was a student. My mother and some of Matilda's friends said that this last period was, in spite of her declining health, among the happiest of my grandmother's later years. I enjoyed her being nearby and often visited on my way home from campus. Matilda attended the parties my roommates and I gave, and sometimes some of my friends accompanied me to visit her. They were fascinated by my grandmother's views and her expressive voice. She read constantly and engaged them in political discussions and lively exchanges about some of the books they had been reading. I particularly remember everyone's admiration for C. Wright Mills. They respected her experiences, and many agreed with her opinions. I was proud of her.

Matilda was born after the Industrial Revolution and grew up breathing the toxic contaminants that mark it. From the coal-burning shtetl and the cities of the east coast to the smog of Los Angeles, the pollutants assaulted her lungs. She suffered from asthma all her life, and she continued to have pulmonary problems in Berkeley, where she was diagnosed with emphysema. She found herself gasping for breath a number of times, and in January 1963 she called an ambulance for the last time. I visited her in the hospital after she had undergone a completely useless tracheotomy that left her unable to talk. "I am a very sick woman," she whispered. I called my mother, who came from Fresno with my brother Dal. Matilda died in 1963, at Highland Hospital in Oakland, on her birthday, January 9.

Although Matilda wrote constantly, the memoir found after her death is the only sustained piece of writing we know of. Many of her sketches and stories are unfinished, and almost everything she finished is short—one thousand words or fewer. Found under the roller of her typewriter was the beginning of an article she was writing for the *Industrial Worker* opposing John F. Kennedy's threatened invasion of Cuba. Beside the typewriter was the beginning of a fictional piece she had begun based on Vita's romance, a quarter of a century earlier, with a young man Matilda found very sympathetic. Underneath the page was a final poem Matilda had written expressing her loneliness and longing for love. Her final essay, published in the *Industrial Worker*, January 23, 1963, was a scathing indictment of the American labor movement and of its representatives among President Kennedy's Council of Economic Advisors. The *Industrial Worker* noted her consistent output in memoriam: "[Matilda] was working on an article about Sacco and Vanzetti . . . and was planning a series of 'personality sketches.'"

An obituary by CC (Carlos Cortez? Charles Curtis?), published in the same issue, described her thus:

> A simple woman, and rather reserved, she would not want effusive displays of mourning. But those of us who knew her will miss her counsel, help and encouragement. She was a valiant in the continuing struggle for peace, freedom and for international

socialism. This is the memory she leaves us, of a life lived mean-ingfully in the service of a great cause.

Matilda was a woman of rare courage. She endured a life of struggle and toil and fought for workers' emancipation during a period where violence against strikers was frequent, but she does not mention feeling fear. She was unyielding in her belief in democratic Socialism and worked with others toward fulfilling those principles. She saw marriage as an institution that confined and abused women and refused to submit to its conventions but was determined to experience sexual connection and the joys of motherhood with dignity, in spite of social disapprobation. Her life was marked by melancholy and regret. She longed for love and connection but was deeply troubled by what she characterized (in personal writings not placed in the Matilda Robbins collection at Wayne State University) as her "monstrous selfishness." While this self-criticism may have prevented her from accepting the love she was offered, she generously showered unconditional love on her grandchildren. It's not the sort of thing one is remembered for, but she was a wonderful grandmother. I am grateful for that.

In her search for beauty, fulfillment, equality, and solidarity with other workers, Matilda represents the many ordinary women that shaped the lives of women today. Although small in stature and self-educated, her knowledge and valor made a profound impression on those who knew her. She maintained her principles, and for the most part her life reflected those values. Although we still struggle with sexual violence, unequal pay for equal work, and challenges to the control of our bodies, today women feel entitled to independence, equal rights, equal pay, sexual and personal autonomy—expectations that Matilda, and the many women who shared her situation and her views, shaped with their courage, labor, and commitment. Vivat Matilda!

AFTERWORD

Ileen A. DeVault

The memoir of Matilda Rabinowitz (née Taube Gitel Rabinowitz) provides us with a unique window into the world of early twentieth century labor. This is true not just because the pantheon of heroes of the Industrial Workers of the World (IWW) has been a male-dominated one, with Elizabeth Gurley Flynn remaining virtually the only woman we know of in this masculinist movement. It is also true because Rabinowitz's memoir gives us an unvarnished, more personal account of what it felt like to live through a tumultuous and exhilarating time in US history. Other labor leaders of that time left us autobiographies—Samuel Gompers of the American Federation of Labor (AFL) and Big Bill Haywood and Elizabeth Gurley Flynn of the IWW, for example—but those works reflect the ongoing institutional ties and justifications the writers sought to present to the public. Matilda Rabinowitz, in some ways more of a professional writer than these more famous individuals, wrote this memoir for a different sort of posterity. We do not know if Matilda ever dreamed that this work would be published. We do know that it gives us a more emotional retelling of a critical time in the labor movement's past than we have ever had before. As Robbin Henderson points out, this personal telling leaves us with some intriguing gaps in the story, usually at moments when even Matilda refused to confront her own pain and agony.

I have been asked to set this work in its historical context and point toward the historical lessons it presents to us. In order to do that, I present a minimalist accounting of three key social movements of that time—labor, socialist, and women's—and how they co-existed within the larger social milieu of the 1910s and 20s.

The IWW was formed in 1905 by a ragtag group of radicals, socialists, and disgruntled unionists in an attempt to provide an alternative organization to the narrow focus of the AFL. The AFL had worked on creating unions of only skilled workers, who were determined to use the economic power of their skills to demand better wages and working conditions from their employers. The IWW, on the other hand, advocated organizing all workers regardless of individual skills or occupations. Heavily influenced by the more radical wing of the Socialist Party of America, the IWW eschewed political action and called instead for direct action at the point of production. This divided its advocates from the political wing of the Socialist Party and the AFL's craft unionists, who believed in careful and controlled efforts through thoughtful and fiscally responsible unions. The IWW, in contrast, believed that power resided, quite literally, in the hands of the workers themselves, unmediated by any organization. This form of syndicalism had already taken root in some European countries, but the IWW became its American form. Like their European cousins, the American syndicalists of the IWW often became entangled in debates over doctrine, within their own ranks as well as among the country's left wing, within the Socialist Party and, ultimately, within and around the Communist Party as well.

Throughout Matilda's story, the Socialist Party plays a continuous role. Matilda's self-identification with the left wing of the party informs the way in which Matilda recounts her story. Even before the outbreak of World War I in Europe, members of the Socialist Party expressed their socialist ideals in varied ways. Some became deeply embedded in electoral politics and, ultimately, in municipal government in particular. Those Matilda and her friends would have called, disparagingly, "sewer socialists," because they were reformist rather than radical, concerned with repairing sewers rather than with more fundamental reforms, ultimately ran cities like Bridgeport, Connecticut, and Milwaukee, Wisconsin, and sent congressmen to Washington. Others within the Socialist Party, including those who helped form the IWW, saw this work as a form of "selling out." These fractures within the party soon came to the fore with disagreements over the war. Although a majority of the Socialist Party voted, in 1917, to support the United States in its war efforts, many of the party chapters, who identified with either the IWW or specific immigrant groups, left the organization in pacifist disgust. Many of these left-wing socialists would, over the course of the 1920s, end up joining the Communist Party (CPUSA). Yes the more top-down structure of the CPUSA also alienated others of the left like Matilda Rabinowitz. From 1919 on, differences between the Communist Party and the Socialist Party created some of the most enduring divisions within the American left and the labor movement.

When Matilda Rabinowitz first became involved with the IWW, she confronted these types of doctrinal fights. During the IWW's first years, most of its efforts focused on transitory male workforces in the western part of the nation. It was only in the early 1910s that the organization and its ideas began to move east into some of the largest industrial centers of the time. The Lawrence, Massachusetts, woolen strike of 1912 and the Paterson, New Jersey, silk strike of 1913 illustrate this. The American Woolen Company was the largest textile firm in the world, with over 30,000 workers in Lawrence; Paterson boasted 25,000 silk workers employed by many different companies. Both employed workforces drawing on the varied and massive European immigrations of the time. As in other textile mills, these workers were overwhelmingly female. They often had arrived in this country with few industrial skills, making them ineligible for membership in AFL unions. Since the IWW had no structure of dues or strike benefits like AFL unions did, these massive strikes of multiethnic workers required great creativity to sustain. This included not only soup kitchens but also tactics like sending strikers' children to live with strike supporters in other towns; in Lawrence, this meant sending them to the homes of middle-class socialists in Boston. Paterson became known for the strike "pageant" that was put on as a fundraiser in New York City. Both of these tactics provide a glimpse of the left-wing "bohemian" movement of the time.

In between these two famous strikes, the IWW sent Rabinowitz to Little Falls, New York, to participate in a much smaller (1,300 strikers), but otherwise similar strike. Rabinowitz's introduction to labor organizing in Little Falls gives us an unusually detailed description of just what such organizing entailed in a time before even telephones were common. Though the author of this work often equates the Little Falls strike with those in Lawrence and Paterson, the strike held less national significance than either of the two larger strikes. In Matilda Rabinowitz's life, however, Little Falls looms large. As her memoir recounts, Matilda took the skills she gained in Little Falls and applied them to other strike situations.

While Matilda herself talks mainly of the socialist and labor movements, she also interacted with the women's movement of the time, most clearly through her interactions with the Women's Trade Union League (WTUL). The WTUL brought together women worker activists and their middle class supporters. While the cross-class nature of the league sometimes created problems for the organization, it also gave the organization a source of funding and support outside of the labor movement itself. The WTUL also gained affiliation with the AFL, which gave it some standing with existing unions but created problems in its relationship with the IWW. Boston members of the WTUL, for example, wanted to assist in the Lawrence strike, but the AFL told them to avoid involvement in this IWW strike. Matilda's brief interaction with the Boston chapter of the league occurred around this time. Her eventual work alongside Marie Hourwich, another Russian immigrant and the daughter of economist

Isaac Hourwich, illustrates some of the pros and cons of the league's cross-class nature. Marie Hourwich, educated at Johns Hopkins, assisted Matilda by employing her, and Matilda, in turn, through her linguistic skills and knowledge of shopfloor issues and culture, provided critical assistance to Hourwich's research.

Matilda's interaction with the WTUL also presaged her continued connection to individuals of greater financial means than herself. In fact, throughout Matilda's activist life we see the ways in which the social movements she participated in were embedded in a larger social milieu that involved both her social movements and coexisting cultural movements. Ben Legére's continued dalliances with the stage place him firmly within the wide-ranging bohemian community of the time. While Matilda does not explain to us clearly how she came to know many of the people who assisted her after the birth of her daughter, she probably met many of them through either their support for labor struggles or their participation in socialist politics and this general bohemian culture. In other words, just as some members of the Socialist Party slid comfortably over to the Communist Party in the 1920s, so the alternative organizations of the 1910s cross-fertilized and provided support for their members.

Matilda Rabinowitz's memoir reminds us that the story of social movements never exists in isolation. Matilda has told us what it was like to be a labor organizer, but a labor organizer who was also an immigrant, a socialist, a pacifist, an unwed mother, an abused partner, and a whole human being living during a challenging time in U.S. history.

APPENDIX FROM THE LIFE OF A
WAGE EARNING MOTHER

I was 29 years old when I decided to have a child. Until then I invoked every means of contraception and worse, so firmly convinced was I that conditions being what they were for wage-earning mothers I had no right to bring a child into the world.

I had seen the burdens of such mothers everywhere. I had seen mill women in New England with their infants crawling about them while they were tending looms and spinners and I had seen their children in the gutters of Fall River and Lawrence and New Bedford. The horrible pictures of the children suffering for lack of care were indelibly impressed on my memory. And the chaotic life of wage-earning mothers in our large cities, New York, Chicago, Cleveland, Boston. The spectre of it! No, I would not subject a child to it.

I had no husband to depend on; I sensed no particular urge to be a mother, and I held fast to my theory that as long as women are compelled to be wage-earners as well as mothers, motherhood was possible only at a terrific price to both mother and child. So argued I for years and for years resisted.

Then, even as I was still arguing that intelligent women had no right to bring children into a social chaos, there came over me a strange mood, an overwhelming, unconquerable desire to have a child. In vain my theories about economic insecurity; in vain my attempts to be reasonable. Nothing could dispel the powerful relentless feeling for motherhood that held me in its grip.

I cannot describe the joy and the peace that came to me during pregnancy. The dignity and courage that I felt! Life took on new meaning. Even the daily office grind which I kept up for seven months seemed less irksome. The power and glory of creation was mine.

I had $250 when I left my job. I knew how inadequate this was to take care of me for the remaining two months and meet the hospital expense. The strictest economy and visits with friends helped some. But even then I had to borrow and left the hospital virtually penniless.

Now the baby was here and my dream fulfilled. Reality stalked grimly about me as never before. What to do? I wanted to nurse the child. But that would mean at least eight months without earnings, and I had nothing. I turned to a friend who had more than she needed. She was generous and on ten dollars a week I lived in the country and nursed my baby. My days were filled with work, washing, pumping water, carrying wood, gardening. But how fine the compensations! In her little crib under the maple trees my baby was splendidly growing, and life had a purpose.

But there came all too soon the inevitable return to the city and the job. Now my baby was a year old and I could no longer maintain myself and her without a job. I thought of various ways in which I might not yet be compelled to leave her. I applied for resident jobs in schools, in child-caring institutions. I was willing to work for small wages, if I could only have my baby with me. But none wanted a mother with a year-old infant.

The large city where I found myself at the time provided no means other than individual service for the care of children. I found a woman in one of the suburbs, a kindly, competent person, and to her hands I entrusted my child, while I lived and worked in town and saw her weekends.

The agony of the separation was intense during the first weeks.

Then, gradually I became inured to it. I had to, for our lives depended on the job. I could not stop too long, nor think too much. The job demanded my attention. But as it was temporary and lasted only a few months. I found myself after a short vacation with my child again in New York City.

Again a job. But in New York with the high rents and the cost of maid service my wares were quite inadequate. I must find another way and I turned to the nurseries.

I first made the rounds of those closest to the street where I lived. I found them ill-kept charity holes, with matrons of low grade intelligence in charge and lacking the most elementary knowledge of child care. Their questions, their suspicions, their treatment of the mothers who were compelled to bring their children to them! It terrified me.

Then at the suggestion of a friend I applied at a well-known settlement on the lower west side of New York that was reputed to have a good nursery. But after leaving my little girl there for two days I realized that the social service theories of its directors and the actual practices were widely apart. For here, too, were forty children of ages from two to six with whose physical and psychological problems a very young woman with a very limited intelligence and a part-time assistant were asked to cope. It was impossible.

I turned to the few "modern" schools. I tried an uptown Montessori kindergarten, housed in a delightful house, with cultured, smiling ladies in charge, and I found that it was only for the rich, or at least for such as had an income of more than forty dollars a week. At another, now famous, the registrar, a curious combination of virtuous spinster and advanced educator, felt very uncomfortable over the fact that I had no husband. Was I sure that I could carry on the responsibility of my child alone? What if I should lose my job? Besides, there was no vacancy, anyhow. At the next the director felt certain that I ought not to undertake the steep tuition of her all-day school and their scholarship fund was exhausted. And so after many and wearisome visits to such schools I gave up and engaging a mulatto girl at twelve dollars a week to care for my child from eight in the morning until six at night, I did the best I could with my two jobs—one at the office and one after office hours at home.

As long as the maid came regularly and I could get to my job on time everything worked more or less smoothly. But there were at times sudden telephone calls that she would be late, or that she couldn't come at all. In the first instance the nervous condition induced would invariably react on my work in the office. In the second, there being no adjustment of the relentless regularity of the job demand, it had to be suspended for that day, and full of distress and fear for my job I had to jerk myself into the home job. At such times there would come over me the hopelessness of it all: the slavery, the tragedy.

And I shall always remember one agonizing week when my little girl was ill. To leave the sick child in the morning in the care of others; to get to the office in a worried and exhausted state, and to pretend to be normal and calm and efficient, while my thoughts were with the sick child at home—what misery! Of course my work suffered and my health, even as suffers the work and health of thousands of wage-earning mothers.

The summer was coming on and with it the attendant ills of lack of air and space for a growing, running child. Also the daily confinement in the office all day and at home every evening began to tell on my own health and spirits. For the good of both it was necessary to make a change. I found a place about two hours out of New York where for a moderate rate my little girl could board and have the companionship of birds and trees and children and the loveliness of a New England summer.

I saw her every week or two and though the hours were few and the partings hard there was compensation in knowing that my child was away from the broiling pavements of New York, from the congestion and noise and sordidness of the city in summer.

But the summer was drawing to a close and I knew that in the fall I must again fit myself and my child into the city environment. An apartment, a maid for the child—once more readjustment, the double job of wage-earner and mother—the waste of life and health, the futility of it all!

I wanted to continue making it possible for my child to have space and air and sunlight—the need of all growing life for which we city dwellers pay such an exorbitant price, and I began to consider living in a suburb and commuting to my job. And in my desire to provide these essentials, I overlooked some serious disadvantages of such a move.

Within the commuting radius of New York rents are practically as high as in the city. My railroad fare was sixteen dollars a month. I paid as much for maid service as I did in the city and it was more difficult to obtain and keep. And the distress of the inflexible train schedule! That same train every morning, or I could not get to my job. That same train back every night, for the maid would not stay after six-thirty. Like a doom was the daily schedule of getting to the city and back. In good weather and in bad; well or ill—the treadmill of the daily program was relentless.

I paid the maid fifty dollars a month; her hours were from eight to six and no Sundays. So evenings and Sundays there were fires to tend and clothes to mend and the innumerable chores of housekeeping. I was housebound every night and too tired after a strenuous day to enjoy the winter outdoors. And yet, one Sunday of tracking a little sled over hard packed snow, or shaping a snow man to the delight of my little girl, or dreaming by the fire while the soft snow flakes patted the window panes, made the hardships seem less difficult.

However, a year of commuter's life quite convinced me that there was not even a partial solution in it. Indeed, it was more costly, more wearing on health, less possible of recreation and social contact. Of course, it was more desirable for the child. She had sun and air and playground and growing things about her. But she could not have all this were I unable to work, and the strain was too great.

So back again to the city. Back to the cubicles we call home; the parched pavements we call playgrounds; the noise and the hurry and the senseless confusion of values. If one could at least get some intelligent assistance in rearing one's child, as partial compensation for the cramping life in the city! But there is nothing to meet the needs of the thousands of wage-earning mothers in the cities of this country. There are books a-plenty and educators and exponents of "new" and "modern" theories on child culture and here and there a school or a group devoting themselves to these theories, and all that is well and good. But what is there for the mother compelled to leave her child for the job? Nothing but those makeshifts which I have tried and found wanting. So we are buffeted between the demands of the job and the demands of motherhood, an unrelated mass clutching at a compromise here, a makeshift there, a concession elsewhere. Somehow we worry along and the children are growing up.

INDEX

Page numbers in italics indicate illustrations.

Immigrant Girl, Radical Woman was designed in MaiolaPro, with Carter Sans, and composed by Kachergis Book Design of Pittsboro, North Carolina. It was printed on 60-pound Natures Natural and bound by Thomson-Shore of Dexter, Michigan.